I'M BORED ... AGAIN!

I'M BORED ... AGAIN!

SUZY BARRATT
AND POLLY BEARD

ILLUSTRATED BY SAM HOLLAND

BLOOMSBURY

First published 2005

Copyright © Suzy Barratt and Polly Beard, 2005
Illustrations copyright © Sam Holland, 2005

The moral right of the authors has been asserted
Bloomsbury Publishing Plc,
38 Soho Square, London W1D 3HB

A CIP catalogue record for this book
is available from the British Library

ISBN 0 7475 7605 X

Designed by Richard Horne

10 9 8 7 6 5 4 3 2 1

All papers used by Bloomsbury Publishing are natural,
recyclable products made from wood grown in well-managed forests.
The manufacturing processes conform to the environmental
regulations of the country of origin.

Printed in Singapore by Tien Wah Press

ACKNOWLEDGEMENTS

A big thank you to both our families and all our friends for enjoying games with us over the years.

FOR

Tom, Ella and Jojo – PB

Joss and Elmo – SB

CONTENTS

INTRODUCTION 8

INTRODUCTION

We've written this book because so many of you enjoyed the games in our first book, I'M BORED!, and wanted more. So here's another collection of nifty ideas of what to do next when you are all hanging around and kicking your heels. The games and activities are spontaneous and simple and don't need lots of planning, money or sticky-backed plastic.

Inspired by the changes of the seasons and the various festivals that we celebrate, I'M BORED ... AGAIN! is designed to keep the family entertained throughout the year. Essentially it follows the same concept of book one: what to play, how to play it and most importantly, how to enjoy playing it.

We've included games that we remember playing as kids like Tic Tac Lips, and others that we have discovered with our own children such as Family Air Guitar and Howling at the Moon. Although some of the ideas are weather-dependent, most are flexible and can be played all year round. Open up any page for some inspiration. Try a Chinese New Year game during the long summer holidays, or conjure up some Midsummer Magic on a dreary winter afternoon. Knowing the British weather, you are more likely to need a cooling water game in the October sunshine than in a typically showery mid-July!

Some of the games are short and sweet. Others last for days on end. Some are boisterous and energetic, while others are quiet and calming. You decide what's right for you. And we hope that you will enjoy the fun that you can have when you're lucky enough to spend some family time together.

We'd love to know your favourite games or your comments and variations on the games in this book. Please visit our website: **www.imboredbooks.com**

I'M BORED! ...
IN SPRING

BALLET AT HOME

When you are full of the joys of spring and can feel your sap rising, a bit of ballet may be just what you need. Lots of girls and boys like ballet, but if you don't want to go to organised weekly lessons, Ballet at Home might be just your cup of tea.

Appropriate outfits are tights and swimming costumes, with hair tied back a bit too tightly. It's also handy to have a few floaty scarves to waft around. Boys can wear capes and stride manfully with their hands on their hips.

Now put on some music — maybe Stravinsky's Rite of Spring. There's always classical music on the radio if there's nothing suitable in your CD collection.

Begin by bending legs and stretching arms in the air for some warm-up exercises. The back of a sofa is an excellent place to rest one leg and try a little work at the bar. It is important to use words like 'plié' and 'jeté', even if you don't know what they mean.

When warmed up, try jumping in the air with hands on hips and landing as softly as possible. If very advanced, criss-cross the feet in front of one another while airborne. Once full of confidence, turn up the music and attempt a full-scale ballet, leaping off armchairs, balancing on one leg while raising the other to unimaginable heights and dramatically prancing around the room.

Listen to the music carefully and decide what sort of dance and expression fit best. Remember to keep toes pointed at all times, and necks as long as possible.

TOP TIP: For extra authenticity, boys may stuff a pair of socks down their tights if they wish.

LAND THE FEATHER

When you are next out and about enjoying the spring fresh air, collect some feathers. When you get home, blow your favourite feather up in the air, or waft your hands underneath it and see if you can keep it airborne. The bigger the feather, the harder you will have to work. Try flying your feather, without touching it, from one end of the room to the other.

When you have become a qualified pilot in this game, choose an exact spot where your feather must land. Either mark an 'X' on a piece of paper and place it somewhere, or Grandpa's bald head will do just as well. The person who wins best flight of the day gets to choose what's for tea.

MAKING A BOOK

World Book Day is usually celebrated in the UK in early March. In honour of this, here is an activity for children of all ages.

Take a couple of sheets of paper and cut them in half. Put these in a pile, fold the pile in half and put a couple of staples in the fold. You should now have something that looks like a book. Fill your book with a story. Write in it, draw in it and stick in photos or pictures cut out from magazines. Leave the front cover blank until you have finished your story, then decide on a title and a cover illustration.

If you are stuck for ideas, here are a few suggestions to get you started:

- My Favourite Journey. Describe a real or imaginary journey, the kind of transport you used, what the weather was like, who you went with and what you saw.
- My Best Friends. Include photos or drawings of your favourite people. Explain what you like about them, what their hobbies are, and who they are secretly in love with. Maybe one of your best friends is your pet. Draw a picture and stick in a few hairs.

- What I Like to Eat. Draw a picture of your favourite meal, with a page for the starter, main course and pudding. You could add recipes or list any restaurants you like going to. You could also write about food that you will-not-eat-under-any-circumstances-at-all-so-don't-keep-telling-me-to-try-a-little-bit.
- Staying at Granny's House. Draw a picture of Granny and her house. Write about what kind of a person Granny is. Is she cuddly, or strict and scary? Does she spoil you with treats and take you to special places when you stay with her? Is she very forgetful and burns cakes all the time? Does she have lots of gentlemen who would like to marry her? Can she still reach to cut her toenails or do you have to help her?

Keep your completed books in a safe place. They will be treasures to look at in years to come.

THE CHORE JAR

If the house is in need of a bit of a spring clean, this is one to get the whole family helping out.

Write some basic chores on slips of paper such as 'Make all the beds in the house', 'Wash up', 'Do the dusting', 'Clear up the cat sick' or 'Put away the toys'. Write enough chores to keep everyone going for an hour. Also write some un-chores down such as 'Have a biscuit', 'Get 10p from mum for doing your chores well', 'Make a wish', 'Give your most hated chore to someone else' or 'Stay up a bit later than usual tonight'.

Fold up all the slips of paper and put them into a jar. Everyone then takes a piece of paper out of the chore jar, and carries out the instructions. When they have finished a chore, they should return to the chore jar and pick another piece of paper. Continue until the hour is up. Believe it or not, a messy house will soon be transformed into a gleaming palace, with very few grumbles or complaints.

Remember to snap your fingers and start humming 'Just a Spoonful of Sugar' while you clean. Spit-spot!

MOTHER'S DAY TREATS

Mothering Sunday comes at the end of March, and in our experience is usually celebrated by Dad taking the kids on a hasty trip to the garage to buy some overpriced, wilting carnations. We think there is another way to make mum feel special, and that is to let her have a couple of hours to herself, to read the papers, potter in the garden, put on a face-pack and paint her toenails, go abseiling ... whatever she wants. And while she is busy relaxing, her adored family in the kitchen can make something tasty for tea.

Here are three fail-safe recipes that all children and dads can have fun with.

CAKE

You will need:

110g (4oz) sugar (granulated, caster or brown)

110g (4oz) margarine or soft butter

110g (4oz) self-raising flour

2 eggs

Switch on the oven to 180°C/250°F/gas mark 4. Get a large mixing bowl and put in the sugar and softened butter/margarine. Mix together with a wooden spoon until the mixture goes much paler in colour, and light and fluffy. This will take at least five minutes. Use an electric whisk if you have one and then it will only take about two minutes. Keep fingers well out of the bowl when using the whisk or you will spend the morning in hospital.

Break the eggs into a smaller bowl and stir them with a fork so that the white and the yolk are mixed together. Tip about a third of the beaten eggs into the large bowl and, using a wooden spoon, beat it really well into the cake mix. Don't worry if it looks a bit like scrambled eggs. Add about one-third of the flour to the cake mix, and stir in slowly. Add the rest of the egg and stir. Add the rest of the flour and mix well.

There, you've done it. Now you can add things to it if you want. A couple of handfuls of sultanas, walnuts or chocolate chips are all very tasty.

Find a round cake tin, about 20cm (8in) across. Get some butter on your fingers and smear a thin layer all over the inside of the tin to stop the cake from sticking. Spoon the cake mix into the tin, pat it down a bit, but don't worry about getting it flat or touching the sides as it will spread and rise in the oven. If you prefer you can make twelve small cakes using a bun tin or little paper cases.

Lick the bowl and wooden spoon until clean.

Cook the cake on a shelf in the middle of the oven for about fifteen minutes (ten minutes for the little cakes) and then take it out and have a look. If the cake looks golden and is coming away from the sides, it is done. Press lightly on the top in the middle, and if it feels firm and springy, then it is ready. If you are not quite sure, then pop it back in for a few minutes longer but check again every two minutes.

When out of the oven, let the cake cool slightly. Turn it out of the tin, and rest it on a wire rack. When completely cooled, top with melted chocolate or icing.

For a really simple icing, put a couple of large spoonfuls

of icing sugar into a bowl and add about a teaspoon of water, lemon or orange juice. Add a drop of food colouring if you like. Mix it into a paste, adding a little more liquid or icing sugar as required. Spread it on the top of the cake letting it drip down the sides. Or you could use shop-bought-ready-made icing, which has the texture of plasticine and is fantastic for making letters, shapes and figures, or just playing with.

Stick on sweets, toy soldiers, flowers or farm animals for extra decoration.

It really is a great feeling to serve up a home-made cake, and all mums will appreciate the time and effort you have put into it. Much nicer than a drooping bunch of pink flowers.

BISCUITS

If you are feeling less adventurous, try making biscuits as they are much easier than a cake. All you have to remember is that biscuit-making is more about cutting out shapes and playing with the mixture than the end result.

You will need:
110g (4oz) margarine or soft butter
55g (2oz) sugar (granulated, caster or brown)
170g (6oz) self-raising flour

Switch on the oven to 180°C/250°F/gas mark 4. Put the flour and butter or margarine into a large mixing bowl and rub together with your fingertips. The clumps will get smaller the more you rub. Keep rubbing and breaking up the clumps until you have what looks like fine breadcrumbs. Add the sugar and squidge the mixture together until you are left with a firm ball. If it is very sticky, add a touch more flour until it is easier to handle. If it refuses to stop crumbling, add a few drops of water. You can also add flavouring like vanilla essence, a couple of teaspoons of powdered ginger, or a handful of flaked almonds.

Make little balls out of the mixture and flatten them with the palm of your hand before putting them on a well-greased baking tray. Don't put them too close together because they may spread out during cooking. Decorate with sultanas, nuts or glacé cherries. Or you could flatten the mixture and cut out shapes, or make figures like gingerbread men. Animal shapes are good, but legs often get a bit crispy and break off. Stick bits of dough together by moistening the joining parts.

Cook in the middle of the oven for about eight minutes, and then have a look. Some biscuits may be golden and cooked already. Lift them with a fish slice and put them on a cooling rack. Leave the thicker biscuits to cook a little longer. Biscuits burn easily so keep checking them. After about twelve minutes they should all be done. When they are cold you can decorate them with some icing (see **Cake page 20**).

CHOCOLATE CRISPIES

These are the simplest and quickest of all, so even the most faint-hearted scaredy-cats can manage them.

You will need:
1x 100g bar of chocolate
2 tablespoons butter or margarine
3 tablespoons of golden syrup or honey
3 or 4 cereal bowlfuls of rice crispies or cornflakes

Put the butter/margarine, golden syrup and broken-up chocolate into a small pan, and warm gently on the stove, stirring at all times until melted. Put the crispies or cornflakes into a large bowl, add the melted mixture and stir together.

Press the whole lot flat on to a large plate that you have smeared with a little butter, spreading out the mixture. Place in the fridge for about an hour to set, and then cut up into squares. Or you could fill small paper cases with a dollop of mixture and then put them in the fridge.

Easy-peasy lemon squeezy.

WELLY-WANGING

By the end of March birds are singing gloriously loudly, lambs are gambolling around, and the good folk of Dorset are welly wanging.

If you fancy doing the same, here's how to wang your wellies. Everyone should put their wellies on, go outside and find a large space, well away from greenhouses, windows and family pets. Take one welly off and throw it as far as possible while balancing on one leg. Then hop in your remaining welly (much harder than it sounds) to where the other welly is lying and compare whose welly wanged the furthest.

You may look madder than a March hare!

BUS STOP

The table shows columns headed I, M, B, O, R, E, D with rows:

	I	M	B	O	R	E	D
NAME	Ian	Mark					
PLANT	Ivy	Moss					
COUNTRY	India	Morocco					
COLOUR	Indigo	Mauve					
FOOD	Ice-cream	Marmite					
GAME	I-Spy	Monopoly					
CAR	Invicta	Morgan					
ANATOMY	Iris	Muscle					

Perfect for a rainy day, this is a great game for older children. Younger ones can play too, as long as they team up with someone who can write quickly.

Everyone playing will need a pen and piece of paper. Draw five wide columns. Decide on about six categories (e.g. a girl's name, a type of tree, a pop singer, a piece of furniture, a colour, a country). Each player should list these categories down the left-hand column. Now pick a letter (not X!) and write it at the top of the next column. Give yourselves one minute to write in that second column, something in each category that begins with the chosen letter. So a C would give you Clarissa, coconut, Charlie from Busted, chair, etc. When the minute is up, compare answers. Score a point for every original answer that you have. You unfortunately do not score any points for having the same answer as somebody else. Continue playing, with a new letter at the top of each column for each round. The person with the most points wins.

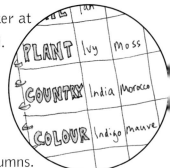

When you get really advanced at this, write a seven-letter word across the top of the page and give yourself five minutes to complete all seven columns.

APRIL FOOL'S DAY PRANKS

There are many differing explanations about the origin of this day. Some say it is to do with calendars, others to do with fish. In ancient times, the first day of April would be celebrated as the day of misrule, when slaves ruled masters and children played tricks on their parents.

The best time to fool people on 1ˢᵗ April is in the morning (it's supposedly bad luck to play tricks after midday). Get up early and prepare some surprises while nobody else is looking:

- Empty the sugar bowl and secretly refill it with salt. Try not to laugh as your family sprinkles it on cereal and stirs it into mugs of tea.

- Remove the inside bag of a cereal box together with its contents and swap it with another one. Just as someone is expecting Shreddies in their bowl, they will pour out Cheerios instead.
- Make a cup of tea for someone, but only use cold water.
- Put the milk in the freezer the night before so that when you try to pour it, only tiny drops come out.
- Get some Sellotape and stick an invisible piece at the top and bottom of the fridge door so that it won't open.
- Write 'Happy April Fool's Day' on a piece of paper. Scrunch it up and stuff it into the end of someone's shoe.
- Choose a road that you walk past on your way to school and loudly declare that Tony Blair or Elton John or Ant and Dec used to live down there. Chances are someone will believe you for a moment, leaving you just enough time to shout 'April Fool!' at them.
- In France, pranksters stick paper fishes onto unsuspecting people's backs. See if you can do the same, but with a message on. For instance, 'I 'm late for work' or 'Tell me I'm gorgeous'.
- Put a hairbrush, apple, or something else a bit lumpy under someone's sheet so that when they go to bed at night they will get a big surprise. Leave a note saying 'April Fool!'

THE DICTIONARY GAME

This is a game full of trickery, so it might be a good one to play on April Fool's Day. It works best with children aged about ten and over, and is a lovely way to while away an evening when there are quite a lot of you. You need at least four of you to make it work.

Each person has a piece of paper and a pen. One person (known as the Sage) also has a dictionary and must search for an obscure word that no one has ever heard of. Let us say for instance that the word chosen by the Sage is 'galloon'. He calls out the word and spells it. If anyone believes that they know the word they can whisper to the Sage what they think it means. If they are right then a new word must be chosen. If they are wrong, however, and nobody knows what the word means, the game can begin.

Everyone makes up a meaning for the word, sensible or silly, and writes it down. False definitions of 'galloon' might be a drink favoured by pirates or a South African wading bird. Just write down what the word makes you think of and add a little detail. The Sage meanwhile writes down the real definition. He doesn't have to write exactly what it says in the dictionary, but just the simple meaning. In this case 'galloon' means a piece of embroidery on the edge of a cloth.

All the definitions are handed to the Sage who, having looked through them and clarified any words he can't comprehend, shuffles them, includes the real definition and reads them out loud. Each definition should be given equal emphasis, as the idea is to fool people. The definitions may need to be read out a second time.

Starting with the player to the left of the Sage, everyone in turn should choose the definition they believe to be correct. When everyone has guessed, the Sage reveals the true meaning. If a player has guessed right, he gets one point. You also score a point each time a player chooses your false description. The Sage receives ten points if nobody guesses the correct meaning.

The dictionary is passed to the left and the next round begins. Keep playing until everyone has had a go at being the Sage.

EASTER

Easter takes its name from the Anglo-Saxon goddess of spring, fertility and the rising sun. Her name was Eastre and legend has it that she wanted to entertain some children one day, so turned her pet bird into a rabbit and got it to lay brightly-coloured eggs everywhere. Now that is a clever trick. Sadly, we don't have quite the same magic powers as Eastre, but here are some ideas to try at Easter that are good fun nonetheless.

EGG-DECORATING

Eggs have played a part in spring festivals for thousands of years. They are given as presents because they symbolise new life, and are traditionally painted to represent the bright colours of sunlight in the spring sunshine.

At breakfast we like to cook soft-boiled eggs, take them out of the water, and paint them as quickly as possible so that the yolk is still runny enough to dip our toast into. We use paint, felt-tip pens, and crayons, which melt and take on their own character entirely.

Patterns that go all the way round the egg such as stripes, zig-zags or circles make an egg look Fabergé-like immediately. If you want a bit more of a family laugh, then draw egg-heads. As well as the obvious eyes, nose and mouth, don't forget beards, glasses, ears, hair, warts and freckles.

EGG-ROLLING

All over the world, egg-rolling competitions are held. If you want to take part in this ancient Easter tradition, you will need to boil your eggs for about twelve minutes. Then decorate it so that you can distinguish your egg from everybody else's.

Find a good, steep hill, and stand in a line at the top. At a given signal, everyone rolls their egg down the hill and runs after it. Eggs tend to take their own path, rather like a supermarket shopping trolley, so if your egg careers off in a wonky line and gets stuck in a ditch you may gently prod your egg with a stick. Hands are not allowed to touch the eggs at any time. The winner

gets an extra hot cross bun. Make sure there is someone waiting at the bottom to verify whose egg made it down first.

If you like this idea but can't find a hill, make a racecourse for your eggs in the garden. It can be up to the shed and back again, round the tree, or in and out of carefully placed obstacles. Lay your eggs at the starting line and proceed to tap them with your sticks, completing the race as quickly as possible.

EGG-HUNTING

The Easter Bunny still visits us, and although some people are getting a bit suspicious about his existence, we like to keep up the pretence.

If you are Easter Bunny this year, here is what is expected of you. Go into the garden and hide loads of little chocolate eggs. If you are hiding big eggs too, put names on them so that each hunter finds just one. They can be hidden anywhere at all but it's best when the eggs can still be seen without having to move anything, so don't go hiding them underneath things. Aim to hide some eggs low down, so that small children can discover them, and some a little higher for everyone else. Find nooks and crannies in

plants and trees where eggs can balance, decorate flowerpots and watering cans with them and locate hitherto undiscovered gaps in the garden wall. They can also be scattered on the lawn.

If the weather is terrible, have the hunt indoors. Balance eggs on bits of furniture, on door handles, in between the banisters, peeping over shelves, or resting on taps or cupboard doors that are slightly ajar.

When all the eggs have been hidden, start the hunt. There are naturally some hunters who are better than others, so if you feel that some people have got way too many eggs, pool them all together in a basket and share them out at the end.

TOP TIP: Dogs are fantastic at egg-hunting. Make sure they don't steal them all.

EASTER BONNETS

These bonnets will not win anyone a prize at the local parade, but they do provide five minutes' peace when everyone's impatiently waiting for that mysterious Easter Bunny to hide the eggs.

Grab a large sheet of newspaper and fold it in half so that the fold is at the top. Take each of the top two corners and fold them into the middle so that you end up with two triangles and a rectangular shape at the bottom. Fold this bottom strip up a couple of times to form the rim of the bonnet, flip over and repeat on the other side. Staple, or stick with Sellotape if needed. Hey presto, an instant Paddington Bear-style hat on to which you can stick scrunched up bits of tissue paper or cotton wool balls, lovingly draw fluffy chicks and spring flowers or simply scribble your name.

Either make your family laugh by insisting on wearing your bonnet (and therefore looking rather silly) for the rest of the day, or take your bonnet off and use it as the perfect thing to collect your eggs in.

PAN-BASHING

If it's a particularly wet Easter, try this noisy indoor game.

Take as many saucepans as you can find, turn them upside down and scatter them around the room on the floor. Blindfold someone with a scarf and turn them round a few times so they become disorientated. Hand them a wooden spoon and ask them to get down on all fours. Secretly and silently, hide a chocolate egg underneath one of the pans. The first player must then beat all over the floor trying to locate the saucepans. Each time they hear a clang, they can lift the saucepan and feel if they have struck lucky. If not, they should continue until the egg has been found.

HANDS AND FEET

It needs a whole big gang of people to make this game work, so we love to play it when our extended family get together during the Easter holidays. It's great to play after a big meal when you are all feeling a bit stuffed full of chocolate.

Get into two teams. The first team goes out of the room, and the second team stays sitting where they can see the door. Then one by one, each member of team A must poke either a hand or a foot around the door (with no clothing or jewellery showing) and wiggle the hand or foot around a bit. Team B must decide who they think it is and write it down. Team A should also keep a note of the correct order, so they don't forget.

The teams swap places and repeat the game. Everyone gets together at the end to reveal their answers and scores a point for each correct guess. The losing team has to do the washing-up.

If there are only a few of you playing, then leave just one person in the room to do the guessing, making sure that everybody has a turn to guess on their own.

TOP TIP: If your feet are as revolting as Auntie Jo's, who hasn't worn any shoes for years and now has things resembling donkeys' hooves, may we suggest you sit this one out.

QUESTION TIME

We love to play this game as a quick filler-in while tea is cooking, and it's great on a car journey too.

One person thinks of an animal in their head, and everyone else must try to figure out what it is by asking questions which can be answered 'yes' or 'no' or 'not sure'.

Here are some questions that will help to reveal the animal.

- Do you have four/two/eight legs?
- Do you have fur/feathers/scales/prickles/a trunk?
- Do you eat other animals/plants/fish/Cheerios?
- Are you very fast/very slow/stuck to a rock?
- Would I like it if you sat on my lap?
- Are you bigger/smaller than our dog?
- Do you sleep in a tree/burrow/underwater/under the duvet?
- Do you roar/snuffle/quack/moo/hiccup?

Everyone keeps on asking questions until the right animal is guessed. Take it in turns to be the thinker-upper.

TOP TIP: Very young children may have to be reminded that they mustn't tell everyone what animal they have thought of straightaway, and that giraffes don't have five legs!

TWO-WORD STORY

The 23rd April is the birthday of Shakespeare, one of the greatest story-tellers that ever lived. Test your narrative skills with this great indoor game. Play with two or more people.

Everyone should think of ten words and write them down on pieces of paper, folded and put into a bowl or hat. The words can be anything at all; the more obscure the better, and can include names of people or places, verbs, nouns or juicy adjectives. Younger children who haven't learnt to write yet can dictate their words to someone helpful.

One person then picks up two words from the hat and begins to tell a suitable tale that incorporates these words. So, let's say the words are 'steering wheel' and 'sheep', then the story may be about a boy who lives on a farm who dreams of the day he drives his father's tractor. You have one minute to talk, slotting in the words as subtly as possible. The story is then taken up by the next player, who picks out two new words to integrate into the tale.

TOP TIP: A minute is a surprisingly long time, so don't think you have to squeeze your words into the same sentence. The story will be much easier to listen to if you spin it out a bit.

SPIES

This game is all about hiding, making sure that nobody sees you get from one place to another, secretly listening in to people's conversations and carrying out dares. You can either play this on your own or in a gang.

Tiptoe around the house finding someone to spy on. Get as close as possible without them noticing that you are there. Either stay crouched just outside their door or, if you're feeling really brave, try crawling into the room and hiding underneath a table or bed, or go behind the sofa. See how long you can remain totally unnoticed, and remember any useful titbits of conversation you pick up — these can provide excellent blackmail material at a later date. If you manage to tie someone's shoelaces together without them noticing, then apply immediately to MI6, who will be happy to employ you as a top spy.

Try adapting this game when you next go on a walk. Adults can walk in front, with any interested spies secretly following them. If the adult turns round to check if they are being followed, the spies must jump into the nearest bush, tree or hedge in order not to be seen. Or they should pretend to be feeding the ducks, stopping to study a leaf or walking in the other direction innocently whistling.

MAY DAY

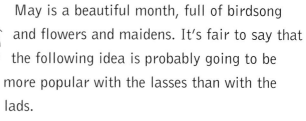

May is a beautiful month, full of birdsong and flowers and maidens. It's fair to say that the following idea is probably going to be more popular with the lasses than with the lads.

On 1st May why not become the May Queen and indulge in a day of pampering. It is said that if you wash your face with the early morning dew on May Day it will give you the softest, sweetest complexion. So get up really early, get outside and rub your face on the grass. Flowers and ribbons are used to decorate the May Queen's hair and clothes, so see if you can fasten a few daisies into a ponytail. If you have ribbons, use them in abundance. Paint toenails a luscious pink, wear a floaty dress and sit around drinking milk and eating honey sandwiches to celebrate the time of year when cows can start to munch long, green grass and bees can start to buzz around the blossoms.

Dancing around a maypole is also where it's at on this day, so if you have a washing-line pole, or a handy tree in the garden, perform a skippity-hop and sing a celebratory song with a hey and a ho and a hey-nonny-no.

BEETLE

There are beetles all over the place at this time of year. Watch out for huge May bugs or stag beetles, which have big antler-like horns.

You'll need to search all over the house for a dice for this game. You'll also need to find a piece of paper and a pencil or a pen that works for each player, which is sometimes just as difficult as finding a dice.

Take it in turns to roll the dice, each player having one throw only before passing it on. You have to throw a one to start, and when you do, you may draw a beetle's body on your piece of paper. Next you must draw a head, for which you must roll a two. Throw a six next to do the tail/sting.

Once the body, head and tail are done you can add, in any order, two eyes (for which you need to roll two fours), two antennae (two fives) and two sets of three legs on each side of the beetle (so you'll need to throw two threes).

If you are the first to complete your beetle, you score thirteen points, and all the other players score one point for each body part they have drawn (so three legs counts as three points). Then everyone starts again on a new beetle. The first person to reach fifty-one points is declared king or queen of the creepy-crawlies.

TOP TIP: This game works best with up to six players. Any more than that and you have to wait too long for your go. Especially if you are three years old.

WHAT THE HELL IS THAT?

Some of you I'M BORED! fans may already have played what we call The Hat Game, and this game is an extension of that, using your very best or worst creative skills to great amusement. As many as you like can play, and all ages too.

Everybody who is playing must write down ten words on separate slips of paper. They can be simple words like 'flower', 'lorry', 'clock' … or they can be more difficult like 'bird-table', 'rain', or 'map'. Occasionally you can put in a real stinker like 'toaster' or 'chocolate chip cookie'. Stick with nouns otherwise it gets really complicated.

Fold up the bits of paper, put them in a hat in the middle of the table, and organise yourselves into pairs or groups.

Decide who is going to go first. They then have one minute to pull out a word from the hat and try to convey to their team what the word is, without saying anything at all.

You can do this in different ways, the simplest of all being to draw your word on a piece of paper. Or, if you have some Plasticine or Play-Doh you can make sculptures of your words, or perhaps hardest of all, tear the shape out of newspaper. This may need a longer time limit. But when time is up you can all shout, 'What the hell is that?!' If your own team haven't got it right after three guesses, then the other teams can try to guess. Score points if you like, and give the younger ones a little longer to complete the task.

CUCKOOS AND COCKERELS

A simple, energetic game for all ages. It can be played just about anywhere except on an aeroplane.

Mark out a line on the floor with string, chalk, rolled-up jumpers, twigs, stones or whatever is to hand. One player is the caller and everyone else stands behind the line. One side of the line is the cuckoo side, and the other side is the cockerel side.

The caller shouts 'Cuckoos!' or 'Cockerels!' and all players must jump on to the correct side of the line. Start off slowly and give young ones an extra chance. When everyone has got the hang of it, the caller should start to call 'Cuckoos!' or 'Cockerels!' more quickly. If you are found to be on the wrong side of the line at any time, then you have to sit out until the next round. The winner is the last one left playing and becomes the caller for the next round.

I'M BORED! ...
IN SUMMER

BIKE RIDES

Summer is made for bikes. They are all about adventures, freedom and going really fast. They guarantee an end to boredom, whether it's just zipping round the block or embarking on a few laps of the park.

Here are some ideas to get everyone out and about on their bikes.

A bike makes a wonderful imaginary horse, complete with clip-clop sounds as you ride along. A helmet, of course, makes a good riding hat. Horses will need tethering every now and then, and given some oats and water before they compete in the Grand National. Or a bike can become a noisy motorbike that roars up the pavement frightening the neighbours' cats (oily rags to shine it up and imaginary petrol are great props here). Or maybe a bike provides the

only means to escape an evil witch's castle where you've been locked up for months dreaming of home.

With the help of a bit of string or an elastic band, a bike can be a taxi service for favoured dolls, teddies and Action Men. We used to dig up worms and drape them carefully over the handlebars, giving them a lift to the end of our street. We then performed what we thought was the most hilarious stunt – speeding around the corner as fast as we could to see how many worms would fall off in one go!

Some eleven-year-old boys that we know like to set up ramps to bike-jump. Prop a plank of wood on a brick and see if you are brave enough to have a go. (Helmets and knee pads are a good idea if you want to do stunts.) These same boys are also very good at having slow bike races, where the winner is the last one to the finish post.

When you get very confident on a bike, there's always the trick of riding one-handed or 'Look! No hands!' to perfect. See how many claps you can do in a row before you get too wobbly, and try lifting up your front tyre wheelie-style. Remember to look cool at all times and to blame your bike if something goes wrong.

FLOWER-PRESSING

A lovely pastime if you feel like a bit of
quiet-time. You don't have to have a
special flower for this. It's easy to do
with some kitchen paper and a couple of big books.

Pick some flowers and leaves. Check beforehand which
ones you are allowed to pick, and avoid wild flowers.
Daisies, dandelions, buttercups and clover are OK though.

Once you have gathered your flowers and leaves, place
them on a piece of kitchen paper and lay another sheet on
top. Carefully put all of this inside a big book – an atlas or
phone directory is good – and place a couple more heavy
books or weights on top. If you have a book that isn't too
thick, you can place the whole thing under your mattress,
but remember not to bounce on the bed while it's there.

After only a few days the flowers should be beautifully
flat and crispy. Pressed flowers make wonderful cards for
great-aunts and grannies, who will sigh and say how much
they miss the old days.

PIRATES

If you are wondering what to do with yourselves on 2nd June, then look no further than a good game of Walk the Plank. This is St Elmo's Day, the patron saint of seafarers. (He also happens to be patron saint of abdominal pains, so if you get tummy ache, he's the one to have a heavenly word with.)

Dressing up as pirates is a great favourite for girls and boys alike. Stripy T-shirts, headscarves, eye patches, a cardboard cutlass and gold hoop earrings are all good. Make a telescope out of old loo-paper rolls.

The boat can be very simple: an overturned chair, a cardboard box, a tree stump, a sofa. Or for a larger vessel, make a den with lots of chairs and tables and tablecloths. Jump around shouting 'Aha me hearties!' and 'I'll have those doubloons!' and 'Oh shiver me timbers, me parrot's flown away again!'

Try playing Feet Off Ground. Think of the ground as

shark-infested waters and place furniture and cushions around the room so that you can leap from one to the other without ever touching the ground and being eaten.

When you need a bit more excitement then have a game of Walk the Plank. Everyone stands in a line, as if you are going to have a race. Imagine planks stretching out ahead of you. Lay a sheet or blanket on the floor where you think the planks should end. Each person should hold a coin in their cupped hands. As everyone calls out 'Yo ho ho and a bottle of rum!' the coins should be shaken in the hands, and on the word 'rum' each person slaps the coin down onto the back of their hand. Anyone whose coin comes up heads must take two steps forward. Tails take one step back. Keep going until everyone has fallen off their planks into the angr' taking their secrets and gold to the bottom of the ocean.

Have fishfingers for tea and tell epic stories of heroic struggles with a giant octopus, discoveries of shipwrecked treasure and surprise encounters with a family of mermaids.

CATERPILLAR-RACING

 In most gardens in summer you will usually find a few caterpillars. If you are in a garden where cabbages, lettuces or nasturtiums are growing, there will almost certainly be loads of caterpillars. Plain green caterpillars and green and brown stripy ones were everywhere in our gardens last year.

A fun thing to do is to collect some in a jar and cover it with a bit of tin foil with a couple of air holes. Make sure you also put in some leaves from the plant that you found them on. They eat incredibly quickly, so you will need to keep an eye on them so they don't run out of food. Once you have been amazed by the amount that they eat (and poo), you can race them. Take a large dinner plate or circular tray, and carefully put the caterpillars as close to the middle of the plate as you can. Then watch to see which little beast makes it to the edge first. You can also try this with slugs, if you can bear to pick them up! Beetles, snails and worms are good too.

When you have finished with your competitors, do not release them back into the lettuces! Find a patch of nettles for them to decimate instead.

TOP TIP: The very hairy brown or black caterpillars might cause a skin reaction, so it's best to leave them alone.

CHEESE AND ONION CHALLENGE

It's a bit of a treat to go to the pub and sit in the garden on a warm summer's evening. We love to play the Cheese and Onion Challenge while we sip.

Get someone to buy at least three packets of crisps, all different flavours. Everyone must shut their eyes while each bag of crisps is emptied onto the table in separate little piles. Hide the bags. Each person takes a crisp from each pile and tries to identify the flavour. If you want to be top-secret about it, you can each write down your answers and compare them later, but it's unlikely that you will be organised enough to have pens and paper with you. So just have a jolly good discussion about it, agreeing or disagreeing and nibbling all the while.

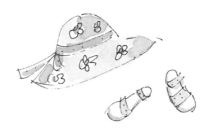

MIDSUMMER'S EVE

Midsummer's Eve falls on the night of 23rd June. For centuries, people have believed that this is the night when the distance between this world and the world of the spirits is the shortest. It is the night when fairies get up to mischief, and magic of all sorts takes place. So here's some magic to try at home.

ABRACADABRA

'And now, laydeezangenmen, will you please give a big Las Vegas welcome tooooooooo … Phoebe and Frankie, the hottest magicians in town!' (Cue: sounds of crowd going wild.) If this sounds like your dream, here are some ideas to put on a magic show to dazzle your audience.

Costume requirements are along the lines of a cloak, a shimmery shirt and tight trousers, and anything with sequins on. Ask someone to be a glamorous assistant, and prance around waving your arms and looking exceedingly pleased with yourself. A wand is essential, and can be fashioned out of some rolled-up paper painted black, and a hat of some kind to produce things from is useful. A table with some shiny paper or tin foil on will complete the look.

Pretend magic is excellent. Hide scarves and other things up your sleeves and then, with a surprised look, pull them out with a flourish. Try hiding a toy rabbit at the bottom of the hat, and cover it with a dark cloth. Show the inside of the hat to your audience, without letting them look too carefully, then plunge your hand in, mutter some magic words (e.g. abracadabra, hocus-pocus or bibbety-babbety-boo), and lift your rabbit up to great applause. Gorgeous assistants can help by looking very impressed and twirling their hands and arms a lot. A lot of magic acts use real animals, so if you have a trusty pet who will do something clever like give you a paw, include them in your routine. Steer clear of white tigers as they might eat you.

But here are a few real magic tricks to try. It's best to have a practice before you show them to an audience. With all of these tricks, it's the way you introduce them that will help to make them a success, so we've added a bit of patter to give you a hand.

LEVITATING COIN TRICK

The power of my mind is growing even stronger, so please stay very quiet so that I may fully concentrate on commanding this coin to jump up and down.

A couple of hours in advance, put an empty glass bottle in the fridge so that it gets very cold. When you are ready to do the trick, take it out and sprinkle a few drops of cold water on to the rim, and a few drops on to a coin, and place the coin on top of the bottle. Stand the bottle on a table and wrap your hands around it. Stare intently at the coin and look as if you are really concentrating. After a few moments, the coin will start to move up and down. When you take your hands away, it may continue to move for a few seconds.

(The reason it does this is that your hands are warming up the air inside the bottle, and warm air expands to push up the coin, but your audience doesn't have to know that!)

AND FOR MY NEXT TRICK ...

Now I will ask my trusty assistant, the beautiful
Madeleine, to help me with this trick.

Your assistant needs to know how to do the trick too.
Ask your assistant to go out of the room, and then invite
the audience to choose any object in the room and tell you
what it is. Call your assistant back in, and go around the
room touching various objects, asking 'Is it this?' Your
assistant will know which object was chosen because you
will make sure that whatever you touch immediately before
the chosen object, will be black. It could be a black
sweater, or cat, or telephone or bag, and the next object
will be the right one. When the lovely Madeleine answers
'Yes!', everyone will try to work out how you did it.

Of course, there are many different ways to play this
trick. It doesn't have to be black, but any colour that both
you and your accomplice have agreed. You could also plan
that as you touch the chosen object you will cross the
fingers on your other hand. Or that you will say '... um ...'
before the chosen object. Or that you will touch all the
wrong objects with your left hand, and the right one with
your right! See how many secret formulas you can come up
with.

MAGIC PEPPER

Prepare to wonder at the power of my mind as I command
this pepper to rise into the air.

On a flat, smooth surface like a plate, put a couple of
teaspoons each of salt and pepper. You need the finely ready-
ground pepper, rather than the stuff you get out of a pepper
mill. Mix the two together and flatten out evenly. Then take
a plastic spoon and rub it on your jumper or the carpet. Hold
the spoon horizontally about two inches above the mixture.
Gently lower the spoon, and the pepper will magically leap
up and stick to the spoon, leaving the salt behind.

UNBREAKABLE MATCHSTICK

Is there anyone here who believes they are strong enough to
break a match? You, sir? Very well, but I shall first cast a
spell on you (… mutter mutter …)

Give your volunteer a normal matchstick, and place it in
one of their hands, so that it is lying horizontally across the
back of their middle finger, with either end poked
underneath their ring and index fingers. However hard they
try it will be impossible for them to break the match. Do
not let them rest their hand on anything.

HERE COMES THE BRIDE

Summertime is full of weddings, and few things are more inspirational if you love wearing princess dresses, tiaras and clip-clop shoes. So why not indulge these desires and organise a home-made wedding.

The first thing to find is the kit: floaty bits of material, fairy wands, pink hairclips, lipstick, a flower for the bouquet, and don't forget the rings. Arrange the room so there is an imaginary aisle to walk up, maybe with a couple of chairs either side. And how about some appropriate music to walk in to, be it classical, brass band, or a bit of Aretha Franklin. Dolls and teddies can be bridesmaids and page boys, and it's perfect if someone can spare a few moments to play the part of the vicar and think up some vows to be repeated.

Traditionally, brides are supposed to have a groom. However, in this game it doesn't matter if the groom turns out to be Buzz Lightyear, Barbie, a willing member of the family (patient pets are excellent), or nobody at all. This is all about being the bride.

If you want the game to continue past the marriage service, don't forget about posing for photographs, sipping from wine glasses and making polite conversation, eating snacks, having a dance, and getting a bit emotional during the speeches.

FAMILY AIR GUITAR

Summer is a time of peace and love and outdoor rock music festivals. If you are feeling miffed that you missed getting tickets to Glastonbury this year, this game is for you. Right, altogether now, a 1, a 2, a 1234! De der de der de der de der de der ...

Yes, you've guessed it. It's time for a bit of Family Air Guitar! Someone finds a good tune to put on the stereo. Obviously anything by Status Quo (a rock band that have been going since Stonehenge was built) is ideal, but you can choose something by Busted, Shania Twain, The Darkness ... anything with a good bit of electric guitar. Surprisingly good are some terrible sloppy ballads from the '80s by Bryan Adams, but you may be too embarrassed to admit to owning such a thing.

Family Air Guitar is for the whole family, with no exceptions. Everyone should grab a wooden spoon, a sieve, ladle, egg whisk – anything vaguely guitar-shaped. Hold low down near your belt, close your eyes, swing your hair and mime playing your guitar. A rapturous look will soon envelop you, and before long you will be lost in the music, and truly believing that you are there, at Wembley, playing to thousands of adoring fans.

Grown-ups look particularly funny doing this, but that is why this game should be tried. Family Air Guitar is played to level everyone out, and get rid of any family tension, and works really well towards the end of the day. If you fancy a change, you can play the Air Keyboards on the edge of a table, the Air Saxophone on your thumb, and for the very weird among you, use a cheese grater for Family Air Pan Pipes.

PERFUME-MAKING

If you are lucky enough to have a garden with some smelly
flowers in it, this is a top activity to while away
a summer's afternoon.

Go round the garden and
check which plants are safe to pick
(watch out for rue and euphorbia
which give you really horrid
rashes) and which plants are not too precious. (Avoid at all
costs the prized blooms that Granny was hoping would win
next week's village fête competition.) Get a bowl and pick
whichever petals and leaves smell the best. Roses, sweet
peas, lavender, rosemary, mint, honeysuckle, jasmine,
fennel and lemon balm are all excellent for perfume. Grass,
daisies, dandelions and weeds are good ingredients if you
just want to make a potion.

Then start creating, with a little water and a few
flowerheads. If you crush the petals with your fingers or
with a spoon, their smell becomes even more intense.

Experiment and play with as many
smelly concoctions as you like. Mix and
match, stir and scrunch. Soon your
mixture will become beautifully

scented. Find a small container and
pour in the watery liquid without
letting in too many of the petals.

Once you have finished your perfume
you should decide on a suitable name
for it. Anything said in a French accent
always works quite well, or something
that sounds passionate and glamorous like 'Symphony',
'Majesty' or 'Intensity'. Then charge a fortune for a few
drops dabbed on the back of the hand.

TOP TIP: Don't let your perfumes sit around because after
a few days they begin to smell like old pond water. A much
better idea is to pour them away and
make fresh concoctions instead.

FORTUNE-TELLING

Now, there are some people who really believe that a little old lady with too much make-up on in a tent can actually predict what will happen in the future. But the truth is, they make it all up, and so can any of us! This is a real favourite, as it combines dressing up, speaking in a funny voice, telling fibs and getting money.

Start off by dressing in a flouncy skirt and a shirt with flowing sleeves (boys too, but without the skirt if preferred). Headscarves are important, and if you can find a couple of clip-on earrings or bangles, they will make you feel even more the part. Make-up, if allowed, should be along the lines of rosy cheeks, red lipstick and maybe a blacked out tooth for authenticity.

The place? Well, if you can set up a tent, all the better. But all you really need is a table with a couple of chairs – one for the fortune-teller, and one for the customer – and, of course, a crystal ball. These are slightly harder to find, but you can use a balloon, or football covered in a floaty scarf.

Tempt your customers by putting up a sign saying 'Remarkable Results with Gypsy Ella' or 'Hear Your Future – I'm Never Wrong'. The more wild the claims, the more

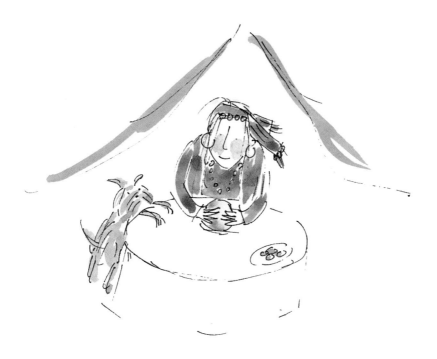

money you can charge. When you have got someone sitting
down, try saying 'Cross my palm with silver so I can
begin.' This means the customer must hand over five pence.

Then the fun begins. Stroke your crystal ball, look up to
the heavens, and do swirly things with your hands. Start to
tell lots of fibs in your best magical voice. Here are a few
good ones to help you start off.

- You are going on a long journey, maybe on four wheels.
- You will meet a tall, dark, handsome stranger.
- Someone is thinking of you right now.
- I see lots of water, maybe the seaside, or perhaps the washing-up needs doing.
- Mrs Wainwright is going to be very boring in maths tomorrow.
- You must share all your sweeties with your sister. In fact, she should have all of them.
- I sense that you haven't done your homework.
- You would like to have a pet dog, but I see a goldfish instead.

When you have finished playing, rest on the sofa with your feet up, count your money, and tell everyone what hard work it is being clairvoyant.

BEACH OLYMPICS

If you are lucky enough to get to a beach this summer, and feel the need for a bit of a runaround, then it is time to organise everyone to have a Beach Olympics.

OPENING CEREMONY

Not strictly necessary, but can get everyone laughing. Choose your nationality. Wrap towels around your shoulders and run along the beach waving at your adoring public. Ask Granny to pretend to be the Queen and welcome everyone. Find a suitable Olympic torch, be it a piece of driftwood or seaweed and pass it from one person to another in a reverential fashion until it reaches the youngest participant who then holds it up to the crowds, who cheer and applaud. At this point, the Beach Olympics have officially begun and everyone should pretend to be a fireworks display. You can all be second-rate rock bands to finish off the ceremony if you wish, but usually by now everyone is ready for a race. Those who don't want to participate at any stage can build sand podiums for first, second and third places, in readiness for the handing out of well-deserved ice-creams and the humming of national anthems.

STRAIGHT RUNNING RACE

If you have lots of people the same sort of age and
ability then this is a pretty straightforward race.
Draw one line in the sand for the start and
another for the finish. Everyone lines up at
the start, the starter shouts 'Take your marks'
... (crouch down on the sand, fingertips
behind a line), 'Get set'... (bottoms up),
'Go!' and everyone runs as fast as
they can to the finish line.

   If, however, you are a motley group of young and old,
big and small, then the starter must position everyone in
different starting places; a long way back for the long-
legged seniors, and only yards from the finish for toddlers.

   Repeat as many times as needed until everybody has had
a chance to win.

RELAY RACE

If you want some more running, then split into teams and
choose suitably beachy batons for each team (a piece of
driftwood, slippery seaweed, a bucket of water, stinky dead
fish). Holding the baton, the first runner in each team runs

to the finish line and back again to the start. He then passes the baton on to the next runner who repeats. Keep going until everyone has had a turn. Mix up ages and running abilities in each team to even things out and scream words of encouragement at your team. Allow the winners a lap of honour.

GYMNASTICS

One of our favourite Olympic events, this is great for pointing toes, keeping your chin up, and looking very proud. Those who don't wish to take part can be judges, giving marks out of ten for each competitor.

Draw a large box in the sand for the floor display. This is the event in which you take big long run-ups and then do triple somersaults in the air. Alternatively you can do a somersault on the floor, or a great leap with legs outstretched. Other good things to do in your display include:

- Jumping, hopping, cartwheels.
- Smiling at the judges.
- Making falls look intentional.
- Running around with a long piece of seaweed trailing behind you, and swirling the seaweed in a big circle over your head.
- Sitting on the sand and wiggling your legs in a bizarre and seemingly pointless fashion.
- Handstands, crabs and star jumps.
- Remaining poised and dignified throughout.

For more advanced gymnasts, try a little beam work. The actions needed are similar to the floor display, but this time, draw a beam in the sand, about two metres long and twenty centimetres wide. Do your best to perform twists, jumps and cartwheels without stepping off your beam. If you fall off, try not to look crestfallen, and hop back on, continuing in a brave way, fighting back hot tears of agony. Dismount, as usual, with a back-flip-sukahara-triple-pike-super-nova.

STEEPLECHASE

First design your track which works best if you are near to the sea. Build a couple of mounds of sand to leap over as if they were hurdles. Then get digging and add some trenches to the course, filling them with as much water as possible. When you are ready to start the race, time yourselves as you complete the course individually, gaining extra points for the most gazelle-like leap or the splashiest jump into a trench.

À LA CARTE ROCKS

This is to be played with shoes on. Find some flat stones and try to balance four or five up one extended arm, imagining that you are a waiter carrying numerous plates back to the kitchen. Mark out start and finish lines and try to run without dropping your stones. If any of them drop you must go back to the beginning. For real authenticity, drape a towel over the other arm and shout out as many made-up foreign expletives as you can.

SOCKHAMMER

Someone has to sacrifice a sock in this game.

Take a sock and fill it half-full with damp sand. Draw a circle about two metres in diameter. Each person plays individually, and must stand in the circle holding the sock in both hands. Then they turn around at least three times, allowing their arms to stretch out ahead of them. When they think the time is right, they must throw the sock as far as possible, taking care to avoid any human obstacles. Competitors must not step out of the circle until the sock has landed. A reliable judge then measures the distance with their feet between the middle of the circle and where the sock has landed, and announces the winner in a tinny voice as if speaking on a bad tannoy system.

BULL'S EYE

Draw a big circle in the sand, then another circle inside that one and a small circle right in the middle so that it looks like a bull's eye target. If you are two years old, stand two paces back from the outer circle; if you are seven years old, stand seven paces back; if you are thirty-five years old then take about twelve steps, while pretending to count up to thirty-five. Throw your stones at the target, and score ten points for the small bull's eye, five points for the inner circle and one point for the outer circle.

If you want a bit of variety, either increase the number of circles, or draw triangles inside the circles. Every time you land on a triangle, points should be deducted. Draw a skull and crossbones too. If you are unlucky enough to land on that, lose all the points you have scored so far.

SHOT PUT

Each competitor makes a ball of damp sand with a small pebble or shell inside it. Hold the ball in the palm of the hand, underneath the chin. Pull lots of strongman faces, grunt quite a bit, look very serious for a moment then launch the ball through the air with a holler and say something like 'woooahhgrpantsski' in your best East European accent.

The winner can either be the one whose ball went the furthest, or whoever made the best noise.

PASS THE BEACHBALL

Surely it is only a matter of time before this becomes an international Olympic event.

Find a spherical object be it a ball, apple or pebble and pass it from one person to the next without using your hands. You can use your feet, knees, elbows, chin, mouth, or anything else you can think of. When you've had your go, run to the end of the line so that you get another turn in a minute. Keep going back to the starting line if you drop the ball and see how far down the beach you can get.

WAIST-DEEP RACE

We don't understand why running in waist-deep seawater is so difficult. It's probably the underlying anxiety of treading on something slimy or crabby that you are not expecting. Anyway, try this great race if you need to tire people out and put those of greater years and ability (granny is the exception to the rule) into deeper water to level things out a bit.

Everyone stands in the sea so that they are waist-deep, whatever their height, with little ones and those who can't swim nearest to the shore and close to a grown-up. Make sure that you are roughly in a line to begin with, and decide where the finish is. When the youngest competitor shouts 'Go!', everyone runs, hands above their heads, to the finishing point.

CRAZEE GOLF

This is a fantastic pastime if you have a ball with you, the smaller the ball the better. It's excellent to play on your own and you don't need a three-iron or any garish  Rupert Bear trousers. Designing and building a crazee golf course is half the fun of this game and everyone will find their own favourite variations, but here are some basic ideas to get you going:

- Imagine you are on the putting green. Dig a hole that is a bit bigger than your ball and then having measured up the lie of the land, roll your ball into the hole. Add a few obstacles such as shells and pebbles if you wish to make the surface more challenging.

- Make another putting green with a mound of sand between you and the hole. Carve a path into the mound to help keep your ball rolling in the right direction.
- When you need a change, flatten the top of your mound, make a hole in the top and roll the ball up at just the right pace so that it rests in the hole.
- Make another mound and tunnel through. Then try to roll your ball through and out the other side.
- Link all the greens together with low walls that will keep a ball rolling in roughly the right direction. Scoop out a few bunkers that you have to avoid.

HUMAN PYRAMID

Not for the faint-hearted! This is extremely strenuous and should only be attempted on nice soft sand, as the chances of everyone ending in a giggling heap are very high. First of all give yourselves a made-up name of a travelling acrobatic group like The Flying Burritos. You may also want to talk in terrible Russian accents while you flex your muscles.

The pyramid itself consists of the four heaviest and strongest people forming the bottom row, the two in the middle of this row standing very close to each other, and all four with their legs apart and slightly bent. Two medium-sized people then climb up on to the bottom row's thighs and balance to form the middle layer. Finally, one small agile person climbs up on top of the middle two to form the top tier

of the pyramid. It's hardest of all on the people in the middle of the bottom row, so don't volunteer yourself for these positions unless you are feeling pretty strong. Or you could have a go anyway and be prepared to collapse and have everyone fall on top of you.

Another variation, which is slightly easier for younger acrobats, is to form the whole pyramid on hands and knees. This gives the upper layers a slightly better platform to balance on. If there are plenty of you then you can make the pyramids even wider and taller, but we've never managed more than three layers plus a small dog on top.

TOP TIP: Elderly relatives or those feeling weak and wobbly should sit this one out!

FRENCH CRICKET

A fitting game to play on 14th July which is Bastille day, when France celebrates its independence. This is a fantastic group activity on the beach. You will need a soft ball and a bat or piece of driftwood.

Everyone stands in a big circle surrounding one player who holds the bat. All the other players try to hit the batsman below the knees by throwing the ball at him. The batsman defends his lower legs with his bat.

The following things may then happen:

- If he successfully defends a throw by hitting the ball, he can reposition his feet to face the next onslaught.
- If the ball goes past him without touching the bat then he is not allowed to move his feet and must execute a clever twist to protect throws from behind him.
- If he hits the ball and somebody catches it, then the catcher becomes the batsman.
- If a player lands a successful hit on to the batsman's legs he gets to bat next.
- All players may stand around shouting 'Sacre bleu!' and 'Vive la république!' whenever it is suitable.

CRABBING

Crabbing off the harbour steps in a Welsh seaside resort is one of our earliest memories. We still love to do it, and are happy to report that our children are just as keen as we are.

You can make your own crabbing lines very easily. A ball of string is all you need, with a weight, such as a stone, tied on the end. A little higher up, tie on a piece of bait (bacon works well), making sure that it will not fall off.

Dangle your crabbing line over the edge of a harbour wall, into rockpools or wherever you think there may be crabs. They will cling on to the bait as you slowly haul them in. Very often they let go just as you are about to get your bucket under them, but keep trying and you will get some.

Once you have caught enough crabs, decide which one is the biggest and which one has been in a fight, and have a crab race. Draw a large circle and stand inside it, either each of you holding your favourite crab (if you are brave enough) or one of you holding the bucket your crabs are in. Count down from three and let the crabs free. Watch your toes carefully and be prepared to get out of the way quickly. Crabs can be alarmingly fast and agile. The winner is the crab that reaches the outside of the circle first.

WHERE ARE MY TOES?

This is very popular with smaller children who need to play quietly for a while and wait for their barbequed sausages to cool down.

One person sits down with their legs stretched out in front of them. Then they cover their legs and feet with lots of sand, doing their best to disguise where their feet are. A small child then pokes a finger into the sand to try to find the buried toes. Be sure to wiggle the toes when they are found. Repeat and swap between the hider and the seeker.

HOT WEATHER GAMES

There are some days in the summer that are blissfully warm. But if the heat is getting to you, here are some good watery games, which will help you to cool off.

MUD PIES

On a hot summer's day, this is a particularly fine and messy way to cool down. You'll need to be out in the garden, and be prepared to get very dirty. Find a patch of earth that  hasn't been planted or used as a cat loo! Dig up some earth with a spade or trowel and put it in a bucket or bowl. Then add just enough water to form a thick, squelchy, sticky lump. Let it ooze through your fingers (or toes!) and add more water or earth until it is the right consistency to make a little cake. Flatten and mould as you see fit, before laying it on a flat surface such as an old plate. As it dries in the sun, decorate it with daisies and dandelions or sticks and stones. You can write letters on the top too, or try to carve a drawing. Hands will get filthy during all of this, so wash them really well before tea, using soap AND a scrubbing brush and no complaining.

SPRINKLER DARES

If you are lucky enough to have a patch of lawn that needs watering on a baking hot day, get out the sprinkler. It's easier than filling up a paddling pool, and loads of fun.

Whack the sprinkler up on full blast and attempt to run through the avenue created underneath the water without getting wet. When you are feeling braver, turn the sprinkler down and try to jump over the water instead. At this point your legs are likely to get soaked, but not too much else. Slowly increase the jets of water and dare yourselves to walk, run, hop or somersault through them. You can also dare yourself to stay totally still and let the jets wash over you once and then back again.

TOP TIP: Move the sprinkler to a fresh patch of grass every so often to stop the lawn becoming waterlogged and too slippy. And have a towel ready in case anyone gets chilly.

THE WATER GAME

Everyone gets wet in this game so don't even think about playing if you want to stay dry. The more who play the better, but we reckon at least four is good.

Everybody except one, who we call the water-bearer, stands in a circle. The water-bearer walks behind the players with a little water in a bucket. He calls out either 'Girls' names' or 'Boys' names', he then calls out a letter of the alphabet, and taps someone on the shoulder. As soon as they can, this player must call out a name of a boy or girl (whichever was chosen) beginning with that letter. Then each player around the circle (going to the left) must call out another name beginning with the same letter.

Play continues, with the water-bearer prowling around the circle, waiting for someone to make a mistake. If anyone hesitates for more than ten seconds, or repeats a name that has already been used in that round, then they get the bucket of water sloshed over them. They may attempt to run away, and it is not unknown for other people to be soaked in the ensuing mayhem. Keep a sense of humour, and remember that, if you are the one who gets it wrong, it is your go next to be the water-bearer.

WORKIN' AT THE CAR WASH ... !

A really superb solution to a hot sticky day and especially popular with dads.

Anybody sitting in front of the television on a hot, sunny day can be given buckets, cloths, brushes, old tea-towels, sponges and washing-up liquid. Yes, it's the perfect time to wash the car. Obviously, if you live in a busy area where you can never park outside your house, this won't be an ideal pastime. But if your car is parked in the drive or on a quiet road, you can spend a good half-hour polishing and sponging the car until it is nearly all covered with soapy bubbles. Then comes hose time.

Some of the soap will come off, some of the spark plugs might get waterlogged, and most scrubbers will end up soaked from head to toe. But there is a great sense of pride in hard work, and you can dance around to sounds of Rose Royce while you clean.

When you have got into the swing of car-washing, you could try cleaning friendly neighbours' cars. However there are a few rules: never ring on their doorbells before eight o'clock on a Sunday, use only fairly dirty water, and make sure there is a cash payment of at least £1.00.

BUFFALOES AND CROCODILES

This is a good thing to do in a swimming pool, but take care with those who are less sure of themselves in the water, and always stop if someone isn't having a good time.

As many people as you like can play this game. Choose one of you to be the crocodile. The crocodile stands on one side of the swimming pool and the buffaloes wait on the opposite side. The crocodile calls out a subject, let's say kinds of ice lolly. The buffaloes then get in a huddle and decide what ice lolly they want to be. Then one buffalo calls out the list of chosen ice lollies to the crocodile. The crocodile chooses one and shouts it out. Whoever's ice lolly is chosen has to swim and run and splash and splutter to the other side of the swimming pool. The crocodile of course tries to catch them, snarling and snapping and being generally cold-blooded and reptilian.

If he is caught the buffalo becomes a crocodile too, until there is only one buffalo left who won't stand a chance! If only a few of you are playing, then the buffalo that gets caught becomes the crocodile, and the croc becomes a buff. If the buffalo makes it to the other side he may either grab a quick nap on the nearest sun lounger, or join his buffalo pals for another round.

JACUZZI BUBBLES

In a swimming pool, or the sea, stand about waist- or chest-deep, and hold your hands above your head. Ask a friend, especially one with big hands, to stand quite close, with one hand either side of you. Their palms should be facing down, about four inches above the water surface. They should quickly push their hands and arms down through the water either side of you. By keeping their fingers together and hands slightly cupped, air will be pushed down to about knee level, and as it rises, you should feel hundreds of little tiny air bubbles brushing past you as they rise to the surface. It may take a couple of goes to get it right, but it's a fizzy thing to do if you are bored in a pool.

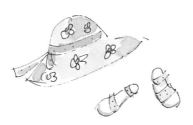

BANK HOLIDAY
BOREDOM BUSTERS

The August Bank Holiday can mean wonderful trips to the beach or visits to friends and family. But unfortunately it can also mean traffic jams, cancelled train services and long queues at the airport. There's a whole section full of journey games to be found in the first I'M BORED! book, but here are a few more for emergencies.

COPY CAT

This game relies on the ability to remember sequences of actions. One person starts by doing an action, such as clapping their hands three times. The next person copies the first action and adds another, so they clap their hands three times and nod their head once. The next player must then clap three times, nod once and wiggle their bottom madly. The next person must clap, nod, wiggle and wedge their fingers in each ear, etc.

This is a good game if you have a bit of space to enjoy yourselves in and even if you are confined to the back seat of a car, it can still be modified to hand and facial movements only. Prizes go to the silliest faces pulled.

CAR-DRUMMING

If you have all got a bit hot and het up, try this idea. It can help to get out a lot of pent-up frustration.

Open the windows. Tune the radio to find some suitable pop music – Coldplay, U2, Phil Collins, Queen and Motown are all excellent, but anything with a solid drum beat will do. Then get drumming, using imaginary drumsticks and an imaginary drum kit with lots of imaginary cymbals and percussion accessories around you. If you have long hair, shake it around in front of your eyes and stick out your lips in a pouty way. Don't forget to twizzle your drumsticks in quieter moments, and do remember to wink rock-star style into an imaginary camera every now and then.

TOP TIP: Try not to hit the seats around you, otherwise drivers and passengers may begin to show their nastier rock-star temperaments.

ONE AT A TIME

Good to play if there are two or more of you, but you do need to be able to spell. To start, someone calls out a letter. Then each person takes it in turns to add a letter in order to spell a word. But you must try not to be the one who completes a word. For instance, if C is called, the next person might say A, (thinking of 'CAT' or 'CAR') but the next person can't say T or R as that will complete a word. So they might say L (thinking of 'CALL'). But the next person mustn't add another L. What about a C (thinking of 'CALCULATE')? And so it goes on, with each player trying to extend the word and catch someone else out. If, when it is your turn, you can't think of a word that fits the letters called so far, then either bluff it by guessing which letter might come next, or challenge the previous person to declare what word he has in mind.

You can make this a winning or losing game if you like, but on journeys it is often better to play for fun and keep those fraying tempers at bay.

TIC-TAC LIPS

A great idea for journeys when there are only a few small sweets around to keep everyone going. We used to laugh so much playing this game – it's something to do with the fact that your teeth and smile take on a whole new ridiculous look.

Hand out a Smartie, Tic-Tac, jellybean or other such sweet to each player. Place the sweet underneath your top lip at one corner of your mouth. When the driver shouts go, everyone must try to get their sweet to the other corner of their mouth as quickly as possible while keeping the sweet underneath their top lip all the time. The best way to do this is to push down on your top lip with your finger. If the sweet drops out from underneath your lip, you have to start from the beginning corner again. Keep racing from one side to another for as long as the sweet holds its shape.

SAUSAGES

This gem is quick and easy and guaranteed to create a few laughs. A perfect ten-minute filler that you can play anywhere.

One of you decides to be the sausage-sayer. This means the only word you are allowed to say is 'Sausages!' Do not say 'Yes', 'No', 'That's not fair!', only 'Sausages!' The sausage-sayer must also keep a straight face throughout. Any twitch of a smile or hint of a giggle and the job of sausage-sayer must be passed to someone else.

Everyone else asks the sausage-sayer any questions they like. For example, 'What's that hanging out of your nose?', 'What do you pour on your cornflakes in the morning?', 'What does your school say to the headmaster every morning?', 'What do you clean your teeth with?' The sausage-sayer must of course answer 'Sausages!' to all such questions in the most serious voice they can muster. Remember, no smiling allowed.

TATTOOS

This is one of our favourite 'hanging around' games. The only thing you need is your finger and a patch of someone else's skin for the tattoo. It's completely painless, by the way.

Decide who is going to have the tattoo done first. They should choose where they would like their tattoo (palms, backs of hands, forearms, knees and backs all work very well) and roll up any clothing necessary to reveal their skin. They should then close their eyes and promise not to peep. The tattoo-artist then draws an imaginary tattoo with their finger. Start with obvious shapes like a flower, a star, a house or a heart. When the tattoo is complete, the person who has been sitting still with their eyes closed has to try and guess what the tattoo is. Repeat the tattoo drawing if necessary and swap roles if you want.

For those who can spell, try tattooing secret messages by drawing letters on each other's hand. Rub your whole hand over someone's palm (as if you were trying to brush off some crumbs) to signify a new word, and be sure to tattoo punctuation marks such as full stops or question marks.

WORD ASSOCIATION

We remember playing this as teenagers, looking up at starry skies on the top of a romantic, deserted hillside. But children of all ages really respond to this and it's a good low-energy game to help pass the time.

Somebody starts by calling out any word that comes into their head. Let's say 'fish' is the first word. The next player thinks briefly about 'fish' and says another word that they consider to be in someway connected to it, e.g. 'gold'. Then the next player thinks about 'gold' and says 'coins' and so it goes on. You are not allowed to repeat words, you mustn't leave too long a pause, and you must be able to explain any weird connections that nobody else understands.

Once you have been around the circle three times, it's quite fun to go backwards and see if you can remember what you all said.

I'M BORED! ...

IN AUTUMN

CUT AND PASTE

Have you ever wanted to have Beyoncé's body? Or perhaps have always dreamt of looking like David Beckham? Can you picture yourself on holiday with a realm of celebrities?

Cut and Paste is a great autumnal activity, using up any photos of your summer holidays that are not required in the family album.

Carefully cut out as many familiar faces as you can and put to one side. Then get hold of a magazine that is stuffed full of celebrity pictures and gossip. Flick through, paying special attention to the size and shape of the celebrity heads on offer, and try to match them up in size with your photo cut-outs. Stick your cut-out heads on to whichever body fits the best. If the celebrity has particularly famous hair, then it's often a good idea to keep their hair and not have any of your photo cut-out's hair showing. Take your time in deciding which cut-out goes where, and trim the photos to get the best possible fit.

Don't just limit it to faces though. An entire cut-out family can look very proud standing on Roger Moore's luxury yacht, or as mystery guests at J-Lo's wedding party or perhaps loitering behind Tara Palmer-Tomkinson on one of her shopping sprees. And doesn't Geri Halliwell look far more fetching wearing your body and bikini?

If you spend some time on this, you can really fool people. Cut and Paste magazines make a fantastic present for someone who needs cheering up. Pretend that it's just a normal celeb mag that you thought they might like to read and then watch their expression as they look inside and realise who the real stars are.

BACK TO SCHOOL

Playing schools at home is very popular. Younger siblings often feel left out when everyone else is dashing off to lessons. Three-year-olds are formidable teachers when

teddy and The Incredible Hulk are the pupils. If an older child is the teacher, they often have infinite patience when it comes

to helping smaller children to read, write and count. However, if you want to avoid a class rebellion, it's a good idea to swap teachers every now and then.

Here are few pointers to get you going. Imagine it's nine o'clock and shake an imaginary bell, shouting 'Ting-a-ling-a-ling'. Everyone should line up into single file and march into a classroom. Whoever is teacher can decide today's lesson, whether it's sums, a spelling test, neatest writing or nuclear physics. Once everyone is sitting down, the teacher can take the register and choose a star pupil to hand out the paper and pens. Pupils must remember to put their hands up if they want to ask a question or say something, sit up straight at all times and form lines whenever they walk from one room to another.

Try holding an assembly when important new school rules can be announced and certificates given out for good behaviour. Playtimes (with clapping songs or a kick-around) are essential when lessons are becoming a trifle dull. They are also the ideal time for the teacher to hand over their job to someone else.

If you really want to go the whole hog, queue up for a well-deserved scoop of mashed potato, cooked carrots and something that's covered in brown sauce. And don't forget that hot sponge with custard for pudding!

BAD EGGS

If the onset of an Indian summer means the weather is inviting enough to be outdoors, here is a fine, energetic game, which requires thinking, running and throwing. There should be three or more of you and you need to have a ball.

One person starts as the chicken, and stands away from the others holding the ball. The chicken calls out a category, something like colours, animals, girls' names or football teams.

Let us say the category chosen is 'drinks'. All the other players get in a huddle and choose different drinks for themselves, and one for the chicken too. The chicken then joins the others and is told by one person what the choices of drinks are. The chicken then throws the ball up in the air, calling out one of the drinks. Everyone runs away except for the person whose drink was called, who must get the ball and shout 'Stop!' as soon as they catch it. If the chicken unwittingly calls out his own drink, the others shout 'YOU!' and the chicken must catch the ball and shout 'Stop!'

As soon as 'Stop!' is called, everyone stands still and faces the ball-holder. The ball-holder can take three steps towards someone (more if they have very short legs), then throw the ball, trying to hit them below the knees. If the ball is aimed at you, you must stand still with your legs together and accept your fate. If it hits you below the knee, you lose a life and get a B. Then you are the chicken and the game continues. If the ball misses you, then the ball-holder loses a life and becomes the chicken. Keep going, adding letters each time you lose a life, so first it's a B, then A, then D, all the way to spell 'BAD EGG'. The game ends as soon as somebody becomes a full-blown bad egg. Suitable punishments must be dished out to them such as pinning down and tickling.

TOP TIP: This works best with a beachball, a soft squishy ball or a beanbag. Definitely not a cricket ball.

HOWLING AT THE MOON

In September, there are often huge harvest moons, so called because the darkness is lit up enough for harvesting to continue right through the night. If you spot a harvest

moon, the following idea is the perfect thing to do.

Our good friend Vickey told us about this, and to be honest we scoffed at the thought, much as you may be about to do. But once tried, Howling at the Moon is a pastime to be repeated again and again, whenever anyone is feeling a bit anxious about exams, boys, girls or life in general.

First, pick your time. It can be twilight or midnight, so long as you can see the moon. A full moon is obviously best, but a half- or crescent moon will also do. Then pick your place. You need to be outdoors, preferably a little way away from buildings, so that you don't alarm or disturb anyone else. If you can get to the top of a hill you will really feel the benefit, and we are also very partial to howling on the beach and listening to the waves break on the shore.

All you have to do is lift your head up towards the moon and make lots of big wolf-like howls. Soon you will all start to feel exhilarated, de-stressed and full of lupine energy. Prowl back home and have a cup of hot chocolate or a suitably carnivorous supper.

CATCHING WISHES

This is one of the most delightful times of the year for going on good blustery strolls. If you haven't tried catching wishes yet, give it a go and see if any of them come true.

All you have to do is run around trying to catch a leaf as it falls to the ground. It's harder than you think, and just as you think you've got it, the wind comes along and puffs it just out of reach again. Keep trying, and when you do emerge triumphant with a golden prize in your mitts, have a jolly good wish. Hmm ... now will it be world peace or a baby rabbit this time?

START WITH A SPLODGE

A game especially popular with under-fives.

Take a piece of paper and fold it in half. Open it up again, and on one side of the crease, splodge on some paint, making sure that it stays good and watery. Use a couple of different colours if you want, and splash on spots, stripes, triangles, squares and the like. Fold your paper back in half again and smooth down all over with your hand.

Open the paper up and study your splodge, turning it on its side or upside down, trying to imagine what it could be if you added on some legs or leaves or ears or an extra bit just there. Grab your paintbrush again and do whatever is necessary to your splodge to accomplish your masterpiece.

TOP TIP: The muckiest, most chaotic, splodgiest attempt that doesn't resemble anything at all can always be turned into an excellent monster with the addition of a few horns, a pair of eyes and a tail.

MAKING A TAPE

Most people take photos or videos of important family events, wanting to capture those lovely moments as childhood milestones are reached. A sound recording, however, is often overlooked which is a huge shame. One of our favourite recordings is of our kids simply in fits of giggles. So get out your tape recorder or dictaphone or any new-fangled digital thingummywhatsit and record each other.

Good things to record are stories, jokes, songs or a home-made, five-minute episode of your favourite TV show with everyone singing the theme tune and attempting to do their impersonations of the characters. Or ask questions like:

- Who is your best friend, and why?
- What would you like/did you get for your birthday?
- What do you like/hate about school?
- What do you like/hate about where you live?
- What would you like to do when you are a grown-up?
- Who do you live with?
- What shall we do today?
- What do you know about sharks/dinosaurs/Baby Jesus?

Make sure everyone gets a chance to be the interviewer.

PITTA PAN BREAD

The 30th September is the feast day of St Honorius, who is the patron saint of bread-makers. If you are in the mood for a bit of mixing, kneading and nibbling, then Pitta Pan Bread is the perfect celebration of this day.

All you need is a couple of handfuls of flour, either plain or self-raising will do. Put the flour into a bowl, add a little water, and mix with a spoon or hands to produce a squashy elastic dough. If your mixture is dry and crumbly, add a bit more water. If, on the other hand it is sticky and runny like porridge, then simply add more flour. Continue adding too much water and then too much flour until you are told to stop mucking about.

Take the dough out of the bowl and play with it a lot, folding, squashing, squidging and pummelling. When well-kneaded, make balls about the size of ping-pong balls. Flatten and stretch them, until they are oval-shaped and about five millimetres thick. Put straight in to a non-stick frying pan on a medium heat and cook for about three minutes each side. You don't need to add any fat. Your mini pittas will brown in places and may puff up a bit, allowing you to split them open at the top and put in some cheese, cucumber, ham, hummus or favourite filling.

LEAF COLLAGES

This is another fantastic autumn afternoon pastime, and good for all ages. Choose a bright and breezy day, wrap up and put wellies on, then head off to your nearest park, woods or heath. Take a plastic bag in your pocket and stuff it with leaves, twigs, grasses, bark, hips, acorns, seed heads and anything else that looks interesting.

When you have roses in your cheeks or it starts to pour with rain, go home. Pour yourself a cup of tea, have a large piece of cake and create collages. Big bits of paper and lots of glue are usually all that is needed, but you can use paint, pens and crayons too if you like. A true autumnal masterpiece can easily be fashioned by painting a tree trunk and branches, and sticking on a selection of leaves.

These magnificent creations usually dry up and go crispy after a week, so then it will be time to go out for another blustery collection and start all over again.

DIWALI

Diwali is the Hindu Festival of Light. It is one of India's most important and popular festivals and comes around the end of October, or beginning of November. Homes are lit up and everyone celebrates the triumph of good over evil.

The next two games will light up your own home, especially when the evenings are dark and gloomy.

TORCH TREASURE

This is a great treasure-hunt if you are feeling fed up about clocks changing and the onset of dark teatimes. If you can, play it outside and enjoy the night sky together, but you can stay indoors, draw the curtains and turn off the lights if you prefer. The darker it is, the more exciting your torch adventures will be.

First, choose some treasure that will be spotted when a flash of light passes over it. Something that glistens or shimmers is ideal – a couple of new coins work well or make anything shiny by wrapping it up in tinfoil. Next choose your hiding-place, making sure that part of the treasure can be easily seen. Switch on torches and start the hunt.

Don't give too many clues, as the whole point is to wander

around with your torch looking for anything that might sparkle. If the treasure-hunters are having no luck at all, scribble a quick map showing some obvious garden landmarks or pieces of furniture, and draw a large cross where the treasure is hidden. Unrolling the map, reading it with a torch and deciphering it is a game in itself.

HAND SHADOWS

Position a lamp or a torch so that it lights up an empty wall. Put your hands in front of it in various positions and experiment with the shadows you can make. Don't just stick to the usual bird flapping its wings or rabbit with two long ears. Move your fingers and arms into different shapes and you will soon find yourself with tarantulas, pigs, snails, witches with hooky noses, panting dogs or revolvers.

Remember which ones work best and invent a story that incorporates them all. Invite your audience to sit and watch you perform a shadow play. If your hands are getting tired or you're running a little thin on inspiration, nobody will mind if the silhouettes of Thunderbird 2, Batman or a toy dagger join in on the action.

If you are playing this at Diwali, make sure the goodie beats the baddie and everyone lives happily ever after.

HALLOWEEN

Dressing up as ghouls, witches and zombies at Halloween is enormous fun. The tradition has come about because 31st October was thought to be the night when the spirits of the dead came searching for a living body to inhabit. Everyone would dress up, looking as scary as possible, to frighten these spirits away.

Halloween never seems to last long enough: there are so many things to do at this time of year. Here are some ideas, which you can do not just at Halloween itself, but during the spare moments of the autumn half-term.

PUMPKINS

Apart from carving pumpkins to make lanterns, try the following to make pumpkin fun last a little bit longer.

Small pumpkins make excellent balls. Do not attempt to play pumpkin football, however, as you will either really hurt your toes or get pumpkin goo everywhere. Instead, find some plastic cups or plastic bottles to use as skittles, and place them on the floor. Stand about ten feet away, roll the pumpkin and try and knock over the skittles. Pumpkins have their own way of rolling so chance plays a bigger part than age and experience.

If you are still in the pumpkin spirit, grab paper and pen and try to draw a pumpkin face with your eyes closed. Draw a big circle first, then imagine where the evil eyes would go, the triangular nose, the crooked mouth, plus any other facial features. When finished, open your eyes and see something truly ghoulish.

APPLE BOBBING

An all time favourite. Grab a bucket or large bowl and fill with water. Throw in some apples and try and pick them out using your mouth only. Hands must remain firmly behind your back. If you're lucky there may be a stalk that you can bite, otherwise the easiest way is to resign yourself to getting wet and pushing the apple all the way to the bottom so that you can sink your teeth into it. Dry off with a towel, or if you are feeling messy go straight into ...

FLOURY FACE

A quick way of making yourself appear ghostly white.

Pile up a mound of flour on a plate and hide a couple of coins inside. Be sure to cover up your tracks so that it is impossible to know where the coins are. Ask each person in turn to hold a knife and cut away a small piece of the flour mound. If a player uncovers a coin, they must stick their face into the flour and pull it out using only their mouth.

TOP TIP: Raw flour tastes horrid, so use your teeth rather than your tongue as much as possible.

CHAMBER OF HORRORS

Prepare for squeals of horror and disgust. A little preparation is needed but it's really worth the effort.

Cut a hole in the bottom of a cardboard box that is big enough for hands to squeeze through. Gather together bits and pieces that will feel like something Halloween-ish when touched but not seen. The end of a wooden spoon could be a witch's bony finger, a quick stroke of a scrubbing brush could be her stubbly chin, a furry teddy could become a huge hairy spider and a cauliflower could be someone's brain. Cold cooked spaghetti works well as intestines and try a peeled tomato as a heart. A rubber glove filled with water and secured with an elastic band makes a great dead-man's handshake.

Once you've found at least ten objects, put them to one side out of everyone's sight. Think up a horror story that includes all the various imaginary items you have found. Lay the box on its side so that the small cut-out hole is facing those willing to listen to the story. Ask them to sit in front of the box and close their eyes while you start the story. When you come to the point in your tale where you can incorporate one of your objects, quietly place the item inside the box making sure that nobody is watching. Dare them to put their hand in to feel the eyeballs (squishy grapes) or severed finger (piece of banana covered in honey) and wait for the screams.

TOP TIP: One time we played this, nobody dared to put their hand in, so we have taken to putting a few treats in along the way for encouragement and reward.

BROOMSTICK-RACING

This is good to play, whether you are dressed up or not.
Enjoy it outdoors where there aren't so many things to
knock over.

Create an obstacle course that can combine some
Halloween forfeits (touching something slimy, pulling a
sheet over your head and making ghost noises, or drinking
a glass of blood-red Ribena as quickly as possible) together
with some physical challenges (jumping backwards, running
to the tree and back, or balancing on one leg for ten
seconds). Find a broom for every witch and wizard wanting
to join in. If there are not enough brooms to go round, then
find any decent substitute such as a mop, rake or big stick.
Mount your broomsticks and complete the course, either all
together or separately, comparing times at the end.

Extra points can be won
at any stage by cackling as
loudly as possible. You
win the race outright if
you can persuade a
family pet to fly on the
back of your
broomstick with you.

TICKLY MONSTER

It may not sound like it, but this is a truly scary game, and should only be played by older children and adults with good bladder control. It needs to be dark outside for this game to be really successful.

First of all, hand out a playing card to each player, making sure that the ace of spades is one of the cards. Whoever gets this card is Tickly Monster. So nobody knows who Tickly Monster is except Tickly Monster himself.

Then one by one, in no particular order and at twenty-second intervals, the players leave the room and start wandering around the house. If you find a light on, switch it off. If you find curtains open, close them. The house must be as dark as possible. After a couple of minutes, long enough to make sure that the house is properly dark, the game starts. Everyone must keep moving slowly around the house, in and out of rooms, up and down stairs, listening out for where the others are. Tickly Monster, when he discovers someone, must jump out on his victim and tickle him, whereupon the victim becomes Tickly Monster as well! The game continues, with all the Tickly Monsters sticking together, swapping tips about where they think other victims are, and generally feeling pleased that they are not in the dark on their own any more.

When there is only one person left to be found, the Tickly Monsters must call out 'Last one!' This means that the final victim, if he has a chance, may hide and try to surprise all the Tickly Monsters by jumping out at them. After the last person is revealed, it's time to put the lights on again, sip some camomile tea, and do a little embroidery in the parlour to calm your nerves.

TOP TIPS: The tickling bit is not really necessary. Jumping out and giving them a fright is the important bit. People inevitably hide in this game, but try not to hide in the same place for too long. There is a rule that if anyone is really too scared to play on their own, they may hook up with someone else. But only in exceptional circumstances. It's supposed to be scary.

5TH NOVEMBER

The history of Guy Fawkes and the plot to blow up
Parliament with gunpowder is something we are all told
about when we are young. It's a great excuse to light a
bonfire, watch fireworks, and eat warming food. Here are a
few of our favourite Bonfire Night traditions.

MAKING A GUY

If you are having a bonfire on 5th November, it's a pretty
good idea to make a Guy.

Everyone has their own favourite way to make a Guy, but
we find the most successful method is to stuff old pairs of
tights with newspaper to make the arms and legs. Tie
together with string and attach to a body made of plastic
bags, again stuffed with newspaper. Use a stapler,
Sellotape, glue or string. Remember, the body doesn't have
to look neat because it will be covered in clothes. Dress
your Guy in old garments, which you are quite sure nobody
wants any more. Check out jumble sales, car boot sales
or charity shops for cheap old clothes. An inflated
balloon makes an excellent head, and this can be
drawn upon or

covered in material. Stick on a
fabric nose and eyes. Hair
fashioned out of string or wool,
and a hat always make great
finishing touches.

Once you have made your Guy,
you can sit him on a chair outside your
house and ask passers-by to give you a penny.
But all too soon the time will come when you must place
him on the unlit bonfire. It seems a strange thing to do
after all your hard work, but hey, it's only a tradition ...
albeit a rather gruesome one! You can keep it or break it.

TOP TIP: You can make models like these at any time of
year, and in many towns and villages there are Scarecrow
competitions. They are called different names in different
regions such as Hodmedods, Tattie Bogies and Mawhinis.
Make sure you choose an appropriately silly name for yours.

MATCHSTICK TOWERS

This is a simple game that can keep fingers occupied for
ages. It's good to play on Bonfire Night when the sparklers
have just run out and everyone needs to get back inside to
warm up a bit.

Find a box of matches and tip the contents on to a table. The first player takes two matches and lays them on the table about one centimetre apart and roughly parallel. The next player picks another two matches and lays them on top of the first two matches at right angles. The next player continues and makes a third layer of matches at right angles to the previous layer. Keep taking it in turns to stack up layers until the matchstick tower eventually tumbles. The person who placed a match or accidentally jogged the table and caused the tower to fall loses a life.

When you feel you have built enough towers, the person with the most lives remaining is the winner and gets an extra sausage in their roll. If you manage to build a tower that uses up the entire box of matches then consider yourselves master builders and have a toffee apple.

MATCHBOX NOSE

An excellent game of skill and snot. And a very good way to pass on chickenpox if you have it!

Take a matchbox and remove the drawer with all the matches inside. Then place the sleeve of the box on the end of your nose and pass it to your neighbour, who must place his own nose inside the other end of the matchbox sleeve, and try to remove it from yours without dropping it. No hands allowed in this game, only the power of your nimble nasal nudging.

If you want to make it more competitive, then whoever drops it loses a life or is out. But we think it's more fun just to see how many times you can pass it successfully between yourselves. Ten times gives you official champion status.

SPIN THE BOTTLE

We remember playing this game at Bonfire Night parties with loads of friends, full of fresh air and baked potatoes. After all the excitement of watching fireworks and running around in the dark, Spin the Bottle is a game which gets more daring each year as players get older and bolder. It is also a game that can get a bit mean, so here is a version which, we hope, will take out the sting, without removing the spark.

On small strips of paper, write down forfeits. All the players who are able to write should do this, and those who can't write should whisper them to someone else to write on their behalf. Choose some from the list below, or invent your own (some nice, some difficult) but bear in mind that you may have to do them yourself.

- Sing a nursery rhyme.
- Tell a joke.
- Stand on your head.

- Smell the feet of the person on your right.
- Kiss the person on your left.
- Go to the kitchen and steal a biscuit for everyone.
- Pretend you are a dog for the next five minutes.
- Collect 2p from everyone.
- Do an impression of one of your parents.
- Nominate someone else to do a forfeit.
- Sit on the loo while it is flushing.
- Spell your name backwards.
- Eat three cheese crackers without licking your lips.
- Put pepper on your tongue.
- Wear your shoes on the wrong feet and skip around the room.
- Be kissed by everyone else.
- Pull out one hair from your head.

When you have amassed a good many forfeits, fold them up and put them all in a bowl. Take an empty bottle and place it on the floor on its side. Everyone should sit in a circle with the bottle in the middle. The oldest person goes first, and spins the bottle. Once it stops spinning, the bottleneck will be pointing at one person and they must take a piece of paper out and do whatever is written.

Be generous. If a very young person can't do what is asked, then give them a hand, or another go. If you draw out a forfeit that requires you to do something for five minutes or more, then the game continues while you are doing it, and you are exempt from doing any other forfeits during that time. Keep the game moving, taking turns to spin. And if there is an argument about who the bottle is pointing at then both people have to do the forfeit.

SIT STILL MUMMY

There comes a time in every parent's day when what is needed is a bit of a sit down, just for a moment. A chance to close the eyes and gather thoughts before the onslaught of the school run, teatime and bath. If there is a pre-school child at home who needs to be creative, why not let them paint your face while you get your half a mo of peace and quiet.

Get some non-toxic paints or, best of all, face paints, and sit still with a cup of tea while junior tenderly dips his little brush in his palette and draws lovely patterns all over your face. It's actually rather a nice feeling, cool and stroky. Offer a little encouragement now and again.

Maybe you could have tiger stripes or panda eyes. Mostly we have found that we look more like an abstract Picasso painting, but that doesn't seem to matter. The point is that someone else has been in charge for a bit and there have been a blessed few minutes' breathing space. Depending on how you look, you may want to wash it off before you go out. If you remember, that is.

SCULPTURE CUPBOARD

Making weird and wonderful sculptures is one of our favourite ways to fill a rainy afternoon. We keep all our bits and bobs together in a cupboard, but your sculpture cupboard could be a box in the garage, a drawer, or even a carrier bag on the back of the door. Like us, you probably have plenty of junk in your house already but we thought it would be good to suggest a list of useful things to collect:

- Egg boxes, shoe boxes, cereal packets.
- Plastic containers and packaging.
- Water bottles, washing-up bottles, lids.
- Loo rolls, paper plates, cotton wool.
- Buttons, beads, straws, corks.
- Scraps of material, string.
- Bits of coloured paper, old Christmas cards.
- Balloons, tinfoil, tissue paper, elastic bands.

When it's pouring with rain, use some glue, Sellotape, a stapler and paint and turn old rubbish into wonderful creations. Rockets are great, as are palaces, cars, trains, robots and of course laser-lectric-piaow-guns. Some of the most interesting ones however are abstract inventions that take form in a free and unique way, to be painted and primped for days to come.

TOP TIP: Don't be put off by the mess – it only takes a second to shove leftover scraps in the bin and anything else back into the sculpture cupboard for another day.

SHOPS

For younger children who are just getting into pretending to be grown up, this game is a lovely way to amble through an afternoon. There are all sorts of shops to decide between, but grocer's and shoe shops are particularly fine.

For grocer's you will need some scales to measure things

out and some newspaper to wrap things in. Things for sale could be rice, pasta, dried beans, cornflakes, vegetables, fruit and unopened tins of stuff. If you are feeling really brave you could sell flour, as long as you don't mind getting the hoover out at the end of the day. You may have a toy till that you can use, but otherwise you can make containers to keep all the different coins in. You can use toy money or real money. If you are playing on a table with a drawer, that makes an excellent till. Remember to say 'Ting' whenever you ring something up on the till.

Lay all your goods out on the table, and when somebody arrives with a shopping bag, ask them what they would like today. Hopefully you will have what they are looking for, but if you don't you can be polite and say, 'I'm not sure, I'll just have a look out the back.' Then come back in and say, 'No, I'm terribly sorry, we should have some in on Tuesday.' Alternatively you can just stare blankly at your customer and say, 'Nah, we don't sell it.' Grocers are very good at idle whistling, so make sure you whistle a little tune whenever you are measuring or wrapping.

Shoe shopping is a bit different. Collect loads of pairs of shoes, all different sizes, and lay out only the left one of each pair, in a couple of neat rows. Then pile all the right-foot shoes at the other end of the room. Your job is to convince a customer to buy the most expensive shoes. Let them try on the left one, then go and find the matching one. Help them squeeze their

feet in, and practise doing up laces and buckles. Make lots of soothing noises about how lovely their ankles look, and press on their toes to make sure they're not pinching. Ask your customer to walk up and down the room. Say things like, 'And how do they feel, madam?', 'Well, they will stretch of course', 'No, the rain won't stain them', 'We haven't got any other sizes in brown, I'm afraid', 'Yes, they are a very popular shoe', 'It's a classic style, you'll still be wearing them in ten years' time', 'Oh, high heels are great in the mud'.

If you sense that your customer has no willpower at all, try to make them buy a new handbag too.

THE HA-HA GAME

This is the perfect post-Sunday-lunch amusement when you are all stuffed full of gravy, roast potatoes and blackberry-and-apple crumble. Head for the roaring log fire, lie down in front of it and veg out.

Position yourselves in a sort of circle so that when you are all lying down, your head is resting on someone else's over-full belly, and you have someone else's head on your tummy. One player then says 'Ha!' forcefully enough to make his tummy go up and down. The player whose head moves and reverberates as a result then says 'Ha-Ha!' as loudly as possible, making the next player's head move. That player then says 'Ha-Ha-Ha!' and so on. It won't take too long for all of you to have terrible giggles, which will mean that all your heads will be bouncing up and down. A great way to digest lunch.

HARRY

Full of confusion and silliness, this is a game for at least four people.

Everyone sits in a circle or around the table. It doesn't matter who starts, but whoever it is (we shall call them person 1) turns to the person on their right (let's call them person 2) and says 'Hey Harry!' Person 2 then says back, 'Hi Harry!' and person 1 says 'Tell Harry!' (which means person 3).

Now person 2 turns to the person on their right (person 3), and repeats the same lines. This continues until someone gets it wrong or takes too long to answer, at which point they must have a spot painted on their forehead. Lipstick is good for this, but you can also use the (cooled!) burnt end of a cork. This person is now named One Spot, not Harry.

So the game continues round but next time that person is addressed he must be called One Spot and not Harry. So the conversation may go 'Hey Harry!', 'Hi Harry!', 'Tell One Spot!' or 'Hey One Spot!', 'Hi Harry!', 'Tell Harry!' The more times you get it wrong, the more spots you get, and the game becomes increasingly confusing, with more and more people becoming One Spot, Two Spots and Three Spots.

You can continue as long as you like, but in our experience, if you get more than five spots, you should drop out of the game and go and get everyone a cup of tea and a biscuit.

CATWALK

If you have a flair for fashion you may want to give thanks
to St Homobonus (what a great name!) who is the patron
saint of tailors. His feast day is on 13th November so
celebrate it with a little garment-making.
Alternatively, play this just before recycling day
when there is plenty of newspaper lying around
the house – you will need lots of it.

The aim of the game is to design
and make a piece of clothing
out of nothing but newspaper
and Sellotape. You will also
need a willing model who
must be prepared to stand still
for a few minutes and then
parade up and down a
catwalk showing off your
creations.

Decide what you
want to make first,
be it a jacket, a
dress or trousers.
For tops it's best

to start with two big sheets of newspaper, one covering someone's front and one covering their back, and sticking them together at the shoulders. For skirts or trousers, start by wrapping a piece of newspaper around someone's waist, and work downwards. Add sleeves, buttons, pockets, collars, torn-off jaggedy strips for that wild-child style, or big cuffs and ruffs for the Tudor look. For a more modern approach, cut holes in inappropriate places and try to make your designer clothes as impractical as possible.

When you are happy with the finished product, put on some loud music and ask your glamorous model to mess up their hair and swagger up and down the room with lips pouting and hands on their hips. A pair of oversized high heels can often help the model perfect their walk. Take plenty of pictures with a flash camera and remember to do lots of air-kissing, telling everyone how fabulous they look, darling.

I'M BORED! ...
IN WINTER

SNAP SNAP OINK MOO

A slightly trickier version of snap for a cold wintry evening. There needs to be at least three of you, but the more the merrier.

Each player chooses an animal for themselves, but it must be an animal that makes an obvious noise, like a sheep, cat, hen, snake or cow. Once everyone is clear about which person is which animal, deal out a pack of cards between you. The player on the left of the dealer turns over his first card and lays it in front of himself. Each player in turn does the same, laying their cards in front of themselves. If anyone turns over a card that matches someone else's top card, instead of shouting 'Snap!' they must both make each other's noise. For instance, if pig and hen make a snap, then pig must 'Cluckcluck' and hen must 'Oinkoink'. Whoever is first to say the other animal's noise gets both piles of cards, and adds them to the bottom of their own pile. Each animal drops out when their cards run out.

It can get a bit boring when only two players are left in the game, so we make these two animals joint winners, and they don't have to go to market that day. All other animals must be made into sausages.

HOME CINEMA

One of the pleasures of a truly cold, wet day is to turn it into a lazy day. If it's the school holidays and you know it's going to pour down all day, then relax, let the rain win, and don't even bother to get out of pyjamas. Check out which films are on the telly or get a video or DVD out, and have an adventure rather than a guilt trip.

If you are feeling particularly creative, build up some excitement by drawing posters and flyers for the film you are about to watch. You will also need to make some refreshments – popcorn (see **page opposite**) and drinks with straws so that you can make that slurpy noise when your drink is about to run out. Rearrange any furniture in the sitting room so that you can all sit down in a row, and draw the curtains. Cut up some paper to make tickets, and make sure everyone who wants to watch the film has got one. When everyone is ready, a chosen usherette should turn off all the lights, tear the tickets in half and shine a torch in the vague direction of the cinema seats. Settle yourselves in and begin the film.

TOP TIP: Pause the film in the middle for a loo break and queue up to buy an ice-cream from the usherette.

POPCORN

We haven't yet met a child who doesn't like popcorn, and making it at home couldn't be easier. Give it a go.

Buy some popping corn from the shops and get out a big pan with a lid. Pour in just enough cooking oil to cover the bottom of the pan and put it over a gentle heat. After about a minute put in enough popping corn to cover the bottom of the pan. It might not look like enough, but trust us, it makes masses. Put the lid on. As soon as you hear the first few pops, shake the pan. Keep shaking, without taking the pan off the heat, until all the pops stop. You may need to hold the lid on. When it's done (it takes about three minutes) tip it into a bowl and sprinkle with salt or sugar.

Once you have made your popcorn, you can get a needle and thread and make popcorn necklaces. Be careful not to prick your finger. Or simply sit down and pig out in front of the video.

SNOWFLAKES

If you are longing for the weather to get really wintry – and we're talking deep and crisp and even here rather than just plain old damp and drizzly – then here's a quick and easy way to conjure up some snowy excitement.

You'll need some scissors for this and a piece of white paper. Cut the sheet of paper into a circle. Fold your circle in half, then in half again to make quarters, then in half one last time to make eighths. Get creative with your scissors to cut shapes and patterns from the edges. Try triangles, swirly loops, diamonds, anything at all. The only golden rule is to make sure that there is some paper left on each of the edges, even if it is only a thin strip. If you completely demolish an edge, your snowflake will disintegrate. When you are happy to stop snipping, carefully unfold your paper. You should be able to open it out into your very own snowflake.

If you make enough snowflakes, there will be a huge pile of tiny white bits of paper on the table and on the floor. Grab a handful and have a pretend snowflake fight before sweeping them up.

TWINKLE TWINKLE

This very simple December car game is just the ticket if passengers are in need of a little festive cheer. Traffic jams and dark afternoons are the perfect conditions.

Look out of the car windows and score a point for every twinkling Christmas tree you can spot. When you get to thirty, everyone can have that sweet or snack that has been promised for the last half-hour.

For more advanced mathematicians, try a rather more

complicated version where you score different points for different sightings. For example, score one point for a Christmas tree, five points for coloured lights in a window or garden, and ten points for a flashing reindeer or snowman. Make up the points as you see fit. Score a hundred points if you see the real Santa trying to squeeze down a chimney.

When you arrive at your destination, decide which display of Christmas illuminations was your favourite. It makes the journey back home much more exciting if you're looking out for it again.

CHRISTMAS

It's hard to be bored at Christmas time, with so much to do and so many presents. But here is a great selection of games to play if there are lots of you and you are feeling full of festive cheer.

LAUGHING BALLOON

A funny game to liven things up a bit after Christmas dinner.

One person throws a balloon up into the air. As soon as it is airborne, everyone must laugh loudly and keep laughing until the balloon comes to rest on the floor.

As soon as it touches the ground, however, everyone must be silent. The nearest person then picks up the balloon and throws it up again and the laughing continues.

Sounds simple, but it's surprising how doing and hearing loud, fake laughter can cause you to giggle for real and not be able to stop.

If you are in a competitive mood, players can be out if they laugh in the wrong place, and the last person left in gets an extra After Eight mint. If the balloon pops, you all have to keep laughing until tomorrow.

NUMBER CLICK

A good game to play when there are at least four of you sitting round a table.

This game will have you in stitches at your own incompetence. Grandpa once laughed so much that we thought he had stopped breathing. Fortunately he was fine, but we hesitate to play it again when he's around, just in case. The weird thing is that it is not an obviously funny game, but once you start to get it wrong it's almost impossible to get it right again, and it seems to be ridiculously amusing.

Go around the table each taking a number in sequence.

So if there are six people you will be numbers 1, 2, 3, 4, 5 and 6. Be sure you know what your number is as it's very easy to forget it.

Now, start a steady rhythm of four beats. On beat one, everyone hits the table with both palms. On beat two, clap your hands. On beat three, click the fingers on your right hand and on beat four, click the fingers on your left hand. So you are all going 'hit, clap, click, click' in a regular rhythm together. You automatically speed up as the game progresses, so start nice and slowly.

Once everyone has got into the swing of the rhythm, the person who is number 1 starts the game off. He must call out his own number (1 of course) on the first click, and someone else's number (2, 3, 4, 5 or 6) on the second click. So it might go 'hit, clap, ONE!, FOUR!' On the next click, person number four must call out his own number first and then someone else's number, so it might go 'hit, clap, FOUR! TWO!' Continue, listening carefully for your number. Everyone does 'hit, clap, click, click' all the way through to keep the rhythm going.

The panic that sets in when you hear your number called is what sends you into a spin, and then the stupidity of not being able to remember your own number, or even how to pick another number up to six is what makes this game hysterical. And you have to do it all in the space of a hit, a clap and a couple of clicks.

If you get really good at this game, or it becomes one of your favourites, you can make it a bit more difficult. Instead of picking a number each, choose an animal sound that consists of just one syllable. So 'moo', 'oink', 'miaow', 'squeak', 'grrr', 'woof', 'sss', 'baaa' and 'spout' (if you are a whale) are all great. Make sure you know what each other's sounds are and only make the noises during the clicks. You might well hear 'hit, clap, SQUEAK!, GRRR!' This is the version that nearly finished Grandpa off.

WINK MURDER

Take as many playing cards as there are players, and select one card to be the murder card (the Jack of Diamonds is our favourite). Mix up the cards. Each player then takes a card and looks at it without letting anyone else see what it is. If you get the Jack of Diamonds, then you are the murderer. Keep your cards safely hidden for the remainder of the game.

Everyone should sit and look at each other, exchanging

smiles and frowns and trying to figure out who the murderer might be. The murderer must wink at someone, but without anyone else seeing. If you are winked at, you must wait for about five seconds, then fall to the floor clutching at your throat, and give a very good death scene. You must not reveal who has winked at you. The game continues, with the murderer winking at as many people as he can until there is only one victim left. He must try to wink at them before they have time to accuse him.

If at any point during the game the murderer is spotted winking, he may be accused as soon as someone has died. If you accuse incorrectly, however, you must commit an honourable death by falling on to your metaphorical sword, so don't accuse until you are absolutely certain. Continue long enough for everyone to have had a chance to be the winker.

THE GAME

Everyone has a version of this perennial favourite miming game. We often play it on Boxing Day, feeling a bit sick, full of too many Walnut Whips and yet another helping of mince pies. If you can prise yourself out of the sofa it might burn off a few calories. Play in teams or individually. The game starts by somebody whispering a book title, song, film, play or TV programme to the first mimer. Then, against the clock, the mimer must try to let everyone know what has been whispered without making a sound themselves.

There are various helpful actions to assist you. Here are some of them.

To indicate:

- Film – put one hand around your eye like a telescope and do a winding action by your ear with your other hand.
- Book – place your hands together in front of you and open them like a book.
- Play – make the shape of theatre curtains opening in

front of you.
- TV programme – draw a square shape in the air.
- Song – draw a circle in the air.
- Opera – make grand, over-dramatic gestures, with your mouth open and wobbly.

Other useful actions are:

- To indicate the number of words in the title, hold up the right number of fingers in front of you.
- To break a word down into syllables, place the equivalent number of fingers on your forearm.
- To have a go at doing the whole thing instead of doing individual words, circle your arms as if drawing an enormous globe in front of you.
- For little words like 'the, a, in, to, of, and, if', hold up one hand with a little gap between your thumb and forefinger, and then encourage the guessers to call out little words until they get it right.

You can do the words in any order, choosing the most helpful or easiest words first if you like. Those people guessing must call out what their answers are and if they're right, give them a thumbs-up signal.

If you are playing in teams, act out a title, chosen by your opposition, to your own team only who must try to guess it as quickly as possible. A correct guess within thirty seconds earns three points, within a minute gets two points, and within two minutes scores one point. If playing with very young children, random points can also be given for effort.

If playing individually, act to everyone, and whoever guesses the title takes the next turn.

TOP TIP: Some people, like Joss, cannot bear being made to get up in front of everyone and 'have to do acting', and might actually cry if made to. Hey, it's Christmas ... let them watch the Bond movie instead.

PIG

Did you know that the 28th December is the unluckiest day of the year? So why not test your luck and play Pig. It's full of chance, daring and suspense. You will need to find a dice – maybe someone got one in a new game for Christmas!

You can play with two or more players. The first player rolls the dice, adding up their score as they go. But if they roll a one, they lose their score for that turn and pass the dice on to the next player. They keep on rolling for as long as they want, daring to have just one more throw to try to increase their score. As soon as they want, they can stop rolling, write down their score, and pass the dice to the next player. That score is then safe, and cannot be lost on subsequent turns.

The first player to reach a total of a 101 points is declared the winner, and gets £1 million from all the other players (optional).

NEW YEAR'S DAY PICNIC

It might be hard to persuade everyone to join in with this, as some grown-ups may be feeling a little delicate. Never mind – assure them that a winter picnic is just the thing to cheer them up and blow away the cobwebs.

Pack something nourishing to eat. Our favourite is sausages, cooked just before you leave and wrapped in tin foil to keep them warm, buttered rolls or bread, a thermos of hot chocolate and some satsumas. You can of course take anything you like to eat, but in our experience it's great to have something warm, something sweet and a drink.

Head for your favourite picnic spot or somewhere close to home if the weather's looking a bit dodgy. Wrap up really warm, gloves and everything, and make a promise that you will walk/ run around/ climb trees/ jump off sand dunes/ go really high on the swings for at least half an hour

before you succumb to the delights of your scoff.

TOP TIP: If any grown-ups are looking a bit peaky, tell them to take lots of deep breaths and leave them alone with some water for a while.

NEW YEAR RESOLUTIONS

If, like us, you don't really like thinking up what to deprive yourself of over the next twelve months, try this instead. It may improve not just your year, but possibly your family relationships too.

Every person in the family must think up a resolution for each family member. Some can be tough, some can be funny ... it's up to you.

For instance, resolutions to give to parents could be:

- No shouting at bedtime.
- No shouting at each other.
- Play with me and my toys at least three times a week.
- No swearing at other drivers.

- Ride your bicycle more.
- Don't talk on the phone so much when I need you to take me to the loo.
- Climb trees.
- Learn French so you can help me with my homework.
- Come home from work earlier.
- Stop smoking.

Good resolutions from parents to children include:

- Hang up your wet towel after bath.
- Learn to wipe your own bottom.
- No calling anyone or anything 'stupid'.
- No grunting when you can speak instead.
- Ride your bicycle more.
- Cook a meal with me at least once a week.
- No tantrums in supermarkets.
- Kiss me more often.
- Write a letter to a cousin/granny/friend abroad once a month.
- No teasing your little sister.
- No telling tales on your big brother.

And of course, you can write resolutions for your siblings too:

- No going in my room without knocking first.
- No hogging the computer.
- Hold my hand on the way to school.
- Draw more pictures of ponies.
- Build a den with me.
- Teach me how to curve a football like you can.
- Don't steal the crisps out of my lunchbox.
- No making fun of my spots/voice breaking/body changing.

Aim to take on at least one or two suggestions from each family member and do your best to stick to them for as long as possible. Don't suggest anything too difficult, or it will never be followed through for very long.

This is a good way to start the year: airing your feelings, letting people know how you want to be treated, and finding out how to stop annoying everyone else in your house!

DUVET COVER DRESSING

There are some mornings at this time of year that are so dark and so cold that the idea of getting out of bed, out of pyjamas and into cold clothes is too much to bear. This game provides the simple solution.

Bring your clothes into bed with you to warm them up, and disappear under the duvet. It should be pitch dark under there and very, very warm. Undress, taking care not to let any cold air or light in with careless elbow actions, and redress as quickly as you can, using your sense of touch to guide you. Once dressed and back in daylight, make sure that you have got jumpers and trousers on the right way round.

If you're still freezing cold, hop inside your duvet cover and try one of the following:

- Stick your feet down into the bottom corners, then jump around the room or have a sack race.
- Wrap the duvet cover around your head so only your face is showing. Lie down on the floor on your tummy, keep your legs together and have a caterpillar race, moving your body up and down.

SWAPSIES

The 6th January is known as Twelfth Night, the last day of
Christmas, and traditionally a time for frivolous celebration
and playing tricks. In Shakespeare's Twelfth Night, the
main character, Viola, plays tricks on people by disguising
herself as a boy and gets mistaken for her twin brother.

In celebration of this, here is a game called Swapsies. It
works best in the evening, when getting supper ready and
then all sitting down to eat together. Each person must
assume the identity of someone else in the house. Dress up
in their clothes if you can, wear your hair like them, try to
imitate their voice and the way they walk. Whoever is Mum
must remind everyone to wash their hands, and whoever is
Dad can open the wine. Those people pretending to be the
children must hurry up and finish their homework before
they lay the table. Who should make the salad? Who
should serve the potatoes? Who should tell everyone to
take their elbows off the table? Try to keep
going right through supper, and keep a
sense of humour throughout. Ask each
other how their day has been, and see if
you can imagine what it would be like
being someone else for the day.

At the end of Shakespeare's play most people end up happily skipping into the sunset, but one person is left very upset and has been driven mad. Take care not to drive moody teenagers mad in this game.

BURNS NIGHT

A very popular night with Scottish folk, Burns Night falls on 25th January. It is held in memory and recognition of a poet called Robbie Burns, and is steeped in loads of fantastic traditions. Here is our irreverent, not-very-Scottish version of how to celebrate Burns Night at home.

Your outfit for the evening should be a tartan kilt if at all possible, but we have previously used a car rug, a headscarf, a tartan tablecloth and a shortbread biscuit tin. A bit of tartan somewhere is what counts.

Supper is supposed to be haggis, neeps and tatties. Substitute the haggis with sausages, if you like, tatties are roast or mashed potatoes and neeps are turnips. Boil and mash the turnips. They do have quite a strong flavour, but they are one of those veggies that are exceptionally good for you!

When the food is on the table, it is time to 'address the haggis'. This means give your food a jolly good talking to, and tuck in. During dinner everyone should read or recite a poem. It can be long or short, famous or self-penned. Each poem should be greeted with much applause, and listened to attentively.

After the meal it is customary to dance around some swords. It is possible to recreate this event by placing some ordinary table knives on the floor to form the shape of a cross. Place one hand on your hip, one hand above your head and jig about. Dance in and around the knives until you are hot and sweaty, before calling for a wee dram. This usually means whisky, but you are probably better off sticking with apple juice, unless you want a hangover like Uncle Richard's.

CANDLEMAS DAY

The 2nd February is Candlemas Day and churches throughout the world celebrate with a candlelit procession. Candles are exactly what one needs to brighten up a gloomy February day, so here is a selection of things to try:

- Make teatime a bit different today. Find as many candles as you can, place them around the room, take it in turns to light them all carefully. Then sit down to enjoy a candlelit meal.
- Find a white candle and some white paper, and write secret messages to each other using the candle as your pen. You won't be able to see the message until you take a paintbrush to the paper and wash over it with some watery paint.
- Write a letter to someone, include some very secret information that nobody else should see and seal it with wax. When you have finished writing your message, fold your piece of paper roughly into thirds by folding the top and then the bottom into the middle. The bottom third should overlap with the top third. Take a lit candle and let it drip about ten drips of hot wax at the point where the top and bottom fold meet. Leave the wax to cool (a

gentle blow or two helps), and when the wax is still warm but looks as if it will set any minute, take a pencil and carve out your initial. Don't be tempted to carve too soon. It's easiest to carve in tiny dots close to one another. If you pull your pencil down in a straight line, the wax seal might break.

- Candles go with cake, so use today as an excellent excuse to bake a cake (see **page 20**) and decorate with candles galore. Sing 'Happy Candlemas to Us' and take it in turns to blow one candle out at a time. Make a wish for every candle you blow out.

WARNING: Always have an adult with you if you are lighting a candle.

CHINESE NEW YEAR

The Chinese calendar follows the movements of the moon and therefore starts on a different day every year. Their New Year celebrations usually take place at the beginning of February and provide a welcome distraction to cheer up a rather gloomy time of year. Chinese New Year is packed full of traditions and superstitions, so take your pick of the following and bring a year's worth of good luck to your house.

- Chinese families get together for a ten-course New Year's Eve meal, during which they remember and honour their ancestors. So why not make sure that you all sit down to eat together, have a fantastic slap-up meal that includes rice and chopsticks, and tell tales of your great-great-grandmother or reveal another adventure of terrible Great-Uncle Ken. If there are any old family photographs of when you were all much younger, bring them out, reminisce and laugh at comedy hairstyles and gappy teeth. Don't be too cruel with your comments though, because family arguments, telling people off and crying are to be avoided during Chinese

New Year. They are thought to result in bad fortune and unhappiness for the whole year ahead.

- Wear as much gold or red clothing as possible, as these colours symbolise good fortune.
- Homes are supposed to be scrupulously clean and tidy before the New Year arrives. While we have given up on this task, we do still use this tradition to encourage all the family to help get the table cleared at least. Red envelopes with money inside are given to children after the New Year's Eve feast, so these could be promised if bedrooms are tidied!
- Let the kids stay up a bit later than usual. In China, families play games together well into the night and children are encouraged to stay up as late as possible to see in the New Year. It is believed that parents will live longer if their children stay awake.
- Try not to say or use the number four as in Chinese it sounds the same as the word 'to die' and is thought to be extremely unlucky.

CHINESE WHISPERS

A great game to play after dinner. Chinese Whispers is very popular with very young children and slightly deaf grandparents. You'll need at least four (if it's not too unlucky to say it!) of you to make it work.

Player 1 thinks up a sentence or phrase about a member of the family. Ten words or so with something silly in it works a treat. They whisper their sentence as quietly as possible, and once only, into the ear of the next player. Player 2 should listen carefully, remember the phrase as best they can and whisper it to the next player. The game continues until the phrase has been repeated to everyone around the table. The last person who hears it announces out loud what they have just heard, which will probably be wildly different from the original phrase, which is revealed by player 1.

Chinese New Year is a noisy event with firecrackers going off throughout the celebrations, to scare away an evil monster called Nian. So try the following variation if you want to make Chinese Whispers more challenging. When waiting for your turn, make as much noise as possible by banging your hands on the table, yodelling, clapping as fast as you can or producing an award-winning after-dinner burp.

SNIPPER-SNAPPERS

Snipper-snappers (you'll understand why we call them this when you've made one) are a fantastic way to keep people amused for hours. Make them all year round, but as they involve trying your luck and having your fortune told, they are a perfect activity for Chinese New Year.

To make one sounds complicated, but it really isn't once you get the hang of it. Get a piece of A4 paper and tear off a section so that it becomes a square. Find the central point by folding the square into quarters, then unfolding it and marking with a dot where the folds intersect. Take a corner of the square and fold it so that the tip of the triangle formed touches the central point. Repeat with the other three corners. You will now have a smaller square with four triangles all meeting in the centre. Carefully turn over, and fold each corner into the central point as before, so now you have an even smaller square.

The snipper-snapper is now made. Turn it back over again and you will find four square flaps. Pick the snipper-snapper up by putting your thumbs and index fingers into these flaps and bring all four fingers together so that the inside corners of the flaps meet in the centre. If you push your index fingers away from your thumbs, the paper will open out one way (snipping). Now bring everything back to the centre again and, with fingers and thumbs together this time, pull it open the other way (snapping). Practise snipping and snapping until you get the hang of it.

Now comes the decoration. On each of the four outside flaps, write a different colour, shape, person's name or animal. Try to make sure that some of these have an even number of letters and some have an odd number of letters. Then flatten out your snipper-snapper so that the flaps are on the bottom and you are faced with eight triangles. Starting with the number one, go round each of the triangles and number them in sequence up to number eight. Keeping the snipper-snapper flattened, lift up triangles numbered one and two and write on the back of each triangle a very short fortune. Something like 'You will fall in love', 'You will eat lots of chocolate', 'You will smell like a pig' or 'You will stop waking mummy up'. Continue until all the triangles have fortunes.

The snipper-snapper is now ready to use. Put your thumbs and index fingers back into their flaps and hold the snipper-snapper closed. Ask someone to choose one of the shapes, colours or animals on the outside flaps. Spell out their answer and with each letter, snip or snap. So if they chose RED you would move your fingers three times, BLUE would mean four moves and GREEN would give you five moves. Stay in the final position and ask them to pick one of the numbers that are showing. Snip-snap the same number of times as the number they pick. Do this three or four times, then stop snipping and snapping, lift up the flap that corresponds to the chosen number and read out their fortune. Be sure to sound infinitely wise and bow politely afterwards.

HOT CHOCOLATE

We love this game as it involves chance and chocolate, and it warms everyone up after a bracing, winter walk. Aside from some chocolate, you will need a dice, a plate, a knife and fork, a pair of gloves, a hat and a scarf.

Unwrap the chocolate and place it on the plate together with the knife and fork. Lay out the gloves, scarf and hat next to the plate and sit all who want to play around the table. Take it in turns to roll the dice. If anyone rolls a six, they must put on the hat, scarf and gloves as quickly as possible and everyone else must shout 'Hot Chocolate!' Only when all three woolly items are on can a player attempt to cut off a piece of chocolate, pick it up with the fork and eat it. While all this is going on, the other hungry players continue to roll the dice, trying desperately to get a six. As soon as another six is rolled, everyone shouts 'Hot Chocolate!' and the player wearing the hat, gloves and scarf must stop at whatever stage of the game they have reached and hand over the necessary kit.

Prepare to be lenient with the more impatient members of your family. It's extremely annoying to be denied a piece of chocolate when it is inches away from your mouth.

R AND T

Fathers are particularly good at this pastime. We resort to this game so often to break up any brewing family tensions that we rarely bother to call it by its full name – Rough and Tumble. It can involve a whole variety of games, and the only thing you will need is a soft surface to play on. It does get rough and you will probably tumble at some point. Big double beds are the best arena, as there is plenty of room for the whole family, but a sofa or carpeted floor is fine too. Everyone has to accept before playing that they might get a knock or a bang, but that's all part of it, and tears are rarely shed. No shoes are to be worn at any time. Ensure plenty of tickling, raucous laughter, shrieking and silliness at all times.

Try any of the following ideas:

- Bundle or Human Lasagne – at the spontaneous cry of 'Bundle!' one person (preferably NOT the smallest) lies down. The next person lies down flat on top of them, then the next, then the next until everyone is piled up in layers. Try gently rolling from side to side or see how long the bottom person can endure being squashed.

- Pin Down and Dribble – get someone on to their back, sit astride them and hold down their hands with yours on either side of their head. While they are helpless in this position, make your face loom above theirs and threaten to start dribbling. Never actually dribble, as the consequences can be truly horrible.

- Kung-Fu – always begin by putting your hands together as if praying, and bowing to your partner. Then stand up and pretend to be Jackie Chan as you wave your hands around in a mystical manner, with the odd fast-moving punch or leg kick to follow up. Say things in your best Chinese accent like 'Aaah, so you are the leader of the ketchup spies' or 'Your time has come, my honourable friend' or 'Never forget the power of the jasmine flower'. Don't ever actually hit or kick anyone with a kung-fu move, and always finish the game with a respectful bow to each other.

- Bucking Bronco – a grown-up is the mad bull on all fours. A willing participant then climbs on to their back, holding on for dear life as the bull rears up, jolts unexpectedly, balances precariously on one leg, and generally bucks around trying to make the rider fall off.

- Pillow Fights – these are good breathless fun but avoid direct hits in the face, as they can be a bit nasty. Aim instead for bottoms where you have more chance of surprising someone. Compulsory accompanying noises include 'Hi-yah!', 'Dush!', 'Thwok!' and 'Take THAT you cheeky-beeky!'

- Sumo Wrestling – for authenticity this should be tried wearing your pants pulled high up on your bottom. Stand facing your opponent with hands on knees, staring and psyching each other out. Then wrestle. Hold hands and push each other from one side of the room to another, scoring a point every time you get your opponent's back to touch a wall.

- One-legged Wrestling – balance on one leg, bending the other and holding on to it tightly with a hand. Use your free arm to knock into your opponent and throw them off their balance. If you have to put your leg down at any point to stop yourself falling over, your opponent scores a point. A bell can be rung to start and finish each thirty-second round. In between rounds drink water and suck on quartered oranges. Best of five rounds wins.

PUDDLE-JUMPING

If there has been a good downpour, dress up in as many waterproof things as you can find, and head outdoors. Expendable trousers are a good idea.

Go in search of some puddles. Check the depth of large puddles with a stick first before wading in and splashing as many people as possible. It's a great feeling of abandon to get wet and mucky, as long as you are not too far from somewhere warm and dry.

Puddles that have iced over are especially fun. See if you can you walk slowly across them without breaking them. Be careful not to slip, and be sure to listen out for the great noise when they give a satisfying crunch.

WARNING: Never ever walk on ice on ponds, lakes or rivers.

HUNT THE THIMBLE

When you are stuck indoors and need a game to use up a little energy, but not one that gets everyone too hyped up, look no further than good old Hunt the Thimble.

The rules are simple. All the hunters (and there can be as many as you like) wait outside the room while somebody hides a thimble. Not everyone has thimbles any more, so good substitutes are keys, coins or hairclips. Make sure all the hunters know what the object is. Whatever is hidden must be partly visible without anyone having to move anything.

Invite all the hunters in and let them search, occasionally giving helpful hints about who is closest. Traditionally you say, 'Getting warmer!' the nearer they are, and, 'No, colder. Very cold', when they wander in the wrong direction.

Whoever finds the thimble gets to hide it next go. For a variation, hide a different object for each hunter.

TOP TIP: Watch out when three-year-olds hide the thimble, because they will always say exactly where it is as soon as you walk in the room.

VALENTINE'S DAY

Valentine's cards are so exciting when you really don't know who they are from, keeping people guessing about their mystery admirer for weeks and weeks. If you're worried about your handwriting being recognised, try one of the following top ways to disguise your secret love messages.

- Work out what you want to say, then cut out all the letters of your message from a newspaper. Stick them into your card.
- Try your best joined-up handwriting with the hand you don't normally write with.
- Write each line from right to left with all your letters backwards (try this out on a piece of scrap paper first) so that your message will only make sense when your Valentine reads it in a mirror.
- Use cryptic picture clues and mix with text. So if you want to write 'Be my sweetheart', draw a picture of a bee, then write the word 'my', followed by a drawing of a sweet and a heart.
- Don't write anything at all. Find a photo of yourself that you don't mind cutting up into pieces. Jumble the pieces

up and reassemble them Picasso-style so that one eye is lower than your nose, your chin is on top of an ear, and your lips are on the side of your cheek. When you are happy with your new look, stick the pieces on to a big red heart.

APPLE ANTICS

If you are unsure about who has given you a Valentine's card, an apple might give you a few hints. Take an apple with a stalk. Hold the stalk firmly in one hand and the apple in the other so that you can twist the stalk. Every twist you make counts as one letter, so the first twist is the letter A, the second is a B, the third a C. The letter that you arrive at when the stalk finally twists off is the initial of your love's first name.

Keep hold of your stalk and poke the top of the apple with it, as if you were trying to make a small hole. You will find that the stalk will pierce through the apple skin, but only after numerous tries. Once again, for every poke, count out a letter of the alphabet. The letter you arrive at will give you the initial of your love's surname.

If your apple doesn't have a stalk, then peel your apple skin off very carefully so that it comes off in one long strip rather than in lots of little pieces. Toss your apple skin over your shoulder and look at the shape that it makes on the floor. The letter it most closely resembles reveals your true love's initial.

VALENTINE ALPHABET

This should of course be played on 14th February, but it's too good to play on only one day of the year, so remember to play it on car journeys or waiting in a queue.

Pick a letter of the alphabet for yourself or someone else. Then you must say all sorts of things beginning with that letter. For instance, you begin, ' I love my love with a J because he is Jolly, he wears a Jacket, he lives in Java, he likes to Jump in the air, he doesn't like to Joust with a knight, his favourite food is Jam sandwiches, he works as a Jockey, he keeps a pet Jackal and his name is Jojo.'

Try to include a piece of clothing, something to eat, likes and dislikes, job, pet and place to live. But think up new categories too.

Choose any letter at random or go through the alphabet in turn, and be as silly as you like. The letter X can be tricky, so when you get to that letter you must all give a big Valentine's kiss to the person nearest you. There are no winners or losers, just a great big lovin' feelin'.

PANCAKE DAY

Shrove Tuesday, otherwise known as Pancake Day, comes in late February or early March. Traditionally, the intention of this culinary event is to use up all your extra eggs, flour, milk and butter in preparation for the onset of austere Lent, when such delicious things are off the menu for forty days and forty nights. Most people are not usually very good at giving things up for Lent but are fantastic at eating pancakes, so be prepared to be make them for hours.

For about eight pancakes you will need:

110g (4oz) plain flour
pinch of salt
1 egg
300ml ($1/2$ pint) milk
Splash of vegetable oil (if you add it to
your mixture it really helps it not to stick!)

Sieve the flour and salt into a mixing bowl. Add the egg and beat well with a fork until it's all mixed together. Then add the milk little by little, stirring really well each time, until you have a smooth batter. If it's very lumpy and you have an electric blender then give it a quick whizz. Add the

splash of oil and mix. Heat a little oil or butter in a non-stick frying pan. (A small pan is great, because small pancakes are easier to toss.) When the oil is hot, add a small cupful of the batter to the pan, swirling it round in a circle a few times until the bottom of the pan is thinly covered. Pour any excess back into the bowl. Cook over a medium heat for a couple of minutes, and don't be tempted to turn or toss it until the underneath is really cooked and golden brown. If you toss it too soon it will go all floppy and stick and no one will be very impressed. It's hard to describe how to toss a pancake. All that we can suggest is to give the pan a little shake first to make sure the pancake is not sticking, make a wish, and give it a go. Alternatively, slide a fish slice underneath and flip it over. Let it cook on the other side for a minute or so then pop it on a plate. Squeeze a wedge of lemon or orange over it, and sprinkle with sugar. Roll it up and eat with fingers.

LEAP FROG

The 29th February only comes around every four years, and traditionally girls are allowed to propose marriage to boys on this leap day. But if you don't feel quite ready to get caught up in long-term commitments, then how about a game of Leap Frog instead. It's very fitting to play Leap Frog on a leap day but it is great to play any time you need warming up a bit.

If there are just two of you playing, take it in turns to jump over each other. One of you bends down, legs straight, hands on knees, arms straight, back curved over and head tucked in. The other one takes a bit of a run up and leaps over, by pressing down on the croucher's back with their hands and jumping with legs wide open sideways. You may need to change the croucher's position a bit if one of you is much taller than the other. You may even need to curl up in a ball for very small people.

When there is a whole gang of you playing, then everyone gets into the croucher position in a line, so that the leaper may hop gracefully over each one. When they have finished, they take up the croucher position at the end of the line, and the person who is now at the front can start to leap.

Continue until very puffed and a bit green and croaky.

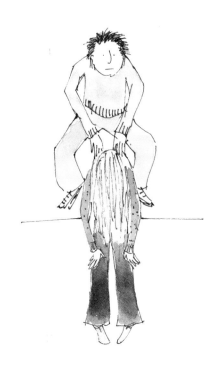

INDEX

NOTE ON THE ILLUSTRATOR

Sam Holland is an actress and illustrator currently living in a small village near Valencia in Spain. She lives with her husband Humphrey and three children Hatty, Tabitha and Penelope, all of whom have provided the inspiration for the family in both books; almost, because the youngest of her children arrived a month after Sam completed the illustrations - Penelope will have to wait for the third book!

NOTE ON THE AUTHORS

Suzy Barratt and Polly Beard are sisters. Suzy lives in Dorset with Joss, Elmo and Lola the dog. Polly lives in London with Tom, Ella and Jojo.

We'd love to know your favourite games or your comments and variations on the games in this book. Please visit our website: **www.imboredbooks.com**